POWER UP! FOR GIRLS

DEVOTIONS FOR GIRLS WHO LOVE SPORTS

DAVE BRANON, EDITOR

Discovery House.

Discovery House is affiliated with Our Daily Bread Ministries,
Grand Rapids, Michigan.

Requests for permission to quote from this book should be directed to:
Permissions Department, Discovery House, P.O. Box 3566,
Grand Rapids, MI 49501.

ISBN: 978-1-62707-492-6

Interior Design by Sherri L. Hoffman

Printed in the United States of America

First printing of this edition 2015

CONTENTS

INTRODUCTION

Every key female in my life has been influenced by sports in one way or another. And that goes all the way back to my mother, who was involved in sports long before the government mandated equal time for girls. She played on a high school basketball team pre-World War II.

Then there was my sister, who hooped it up for a small college in Tennessee when the women still played six-on-six basketball and wore short sleeves instead of tank-top style shirts.

Although my wife didn't play competitive sports, she still reminds me that she did break her arm while playing softball in physical education class. That's a good match for me, because I broke my arm while playing high school basketball. Who said opposites attract?

And this is important: When we began dating, she was quick to point out to me—an Ohio native—who her favorite University of Michigan basketball player was and how many times Michigan beat Ohio State in football. Wisely, I have moved over to her side in this age-old loyalty battle.

Then there are our three daughters, who all kept the sports thing going. At my urging, they all played basketball through the eighth grade, trying to put into practice all my driveway lessons. Although they didn't all continue on the hardwood, they did continue to compete.

My oldest, Lisa, was an ace cross-country runner in high school, finishing 18th in the state as a freshman. My next daughter, Julie, was an all-conference basketball player and a star first baseman on her softball team in high school. In college, she chose to go the intramural route and won lots of free T-shirts as champion in various sports, including badminton, of all things. And Melissa, our youngest daughter, played varsity volleyball and softball. Her name now adorns the softball field at her high school—dedicated in her memory after she died in a car accident on the last day of her junior year.

A few years ago I got involved in girls' sports myself by coaching our high school's freshmen girls' basketball team. I had coached the boys' varsity many years earlier for several seasons, but it was a joy to be working with young women this time around.

I say all that to tell you that just as women's sports and sports-loving women are truly important in my life, they are also increasingly important in our society. Fortunately, there are many women in sports who are followers of Jesus. So if you are a young athlete, that means you have some role models to follow. And if you are a fan, that means you have some top athletes you can identify with and cheer for.

That also allows those of us who write about sports and who attempt to tie sports to spiritual truths to provide you with some articles you can feel comfortable with. Sports mirror life, and we are excited to help you see how sports stories can teach spiritual truths.

In *Power Up! for Girls,* you'll read articles written by some key women who have climbed the sports ladder of success, and you'll also read articles written by women (and, yes, even some men) who are using sports journalism to shine the light of God's truth on life.

During my years as managing editor at *Sports Spectrum* magazine, I always valued the stories of prominent Christian athletes—male and female—and now we're excited to be bringing to you some Bible-teaching, devotionally directed thoughts that can help you, whether you are a female athlete or fan, to see that everything in life—even sports—can be used to glorify God and help you grow in your relationship with Him through Jesus Christ.

—Dave Branon

CLEAR YOUR RECORD

"I, even I, am he who blots out your transgressions, for my own sake, and remembers your sins no more." ISAIAH 43:25

Early in my pro basketball career, I was able to fulfill a dream by purchasing a townhouse. The purchase was one of the most exciting and exhausting times of my life. To be approved for the loan, an officer pulled my credit report to see if I was worthy to receive the bank's money. When the loan officer received the credit report, though, he discovered some delinquent charges that I knew were not valid.

I had to figure out how to clear my name. This rating could cause me to have a higher interest rate. After I went to the sources of the delinquent records and got the correct information, I gave it to the loan officer, hoping it would change the outcome.

Well, it did not! I would have to wait 30 days or more for the changes to clear. Now, that was a dilemma, because I would miss a deal the homeowners were offering. I couldn't clear my own good name.

The amazingly wonderful thing about Christ is this: It is so easy to have a clean record with Him! We are guilty; yet, we can be forgiven. All we have to do is "confess our sins," because "He is faithful and just to forgive us our sins and to cleanse us from all unrighteousness" (1 John 1:9 NKJV). Once you are forgiven, you don't have to wait 30 days for clearance. In Isaiah 43:25 God said, "I, even I, am he who blots out your transgressions for my own sake; and I will not remember your sins" (NKJV).

Ask God to clear your record, and He will say, "Come now, let us reason together. Though your sins are like scarlet, they shall be as white as snow; though they are red as crimson, they shall be like wool" (Isaiah 1:18).

That will get you the home you're really looking for—the one in Glory.
—*Charlotte Smith, former WNBA forward*

GAME PLAN

If you have an open account and have sins that are still on the record, why not stop right now and clear things up with God. Ask Him to forgive you.

From the Playbook:
Read Ephesians 1:3–8.

THE WORD OF GOD

"Do not let this Book of the Law depart from your mouth."
JOSHUA 1:8

According to Joyce Meyer in the book *Battlefield of the Mind,* meditating on the Word of God is one of the most important life principles we can learn.

Meditating on God's Word gives us life (Proverbs 4:20–22). When reading the Word of God, we must understand that it's simply that, a word. But once you begin "to care for," "attend to," "practice," and "study" the Word of God, it begins to minister life to you.

How?

Meditating on the Bible allows the Word to penetrate your soul and plant a seed of life. Not life itself, but a seed of life, within your heart. As you continue to read and meditate on the Word, that word begins to grow. Instruction from God's Word is one of the things the author is talking about in Mark 4:22 when he mentions "the hidden treasure of life."

Once you have revelation from God's holy Word, you then must *do.* You must act. God says, "Do not merely listen to the word, and so deceive yourselves. Do what it says" (James 1:22). Meditating on the Word should lead to action—to doing the things God wants you to do.

Daily meditate on the Word of God, and see how it changes your life. You will discover the secrets to having the abundant life (John 10:10).

—*Kedra Holland-Corn, former WNBA player*

GAME PLAN

When was the last time you meditated on a passage of Scripture, squeezing out God's meaning and then seeing how to put His truth into action?

From the Playbook:
Read Psalm 119:97–104.

A PRAYER TO SOFTEN HEARTS

"Forgiving each other, just as in Christ God forgave you."
EPHESIANS 4:32

Forgiving is tough at times. When others mock you or put you down, the decision to turn your cheek is tough. Our heart's desire is usually to repay evil for evil. But what does Jesus say?

"Forgive [others] when they sin against you" is what Jesus told us to do (Matthew 6:14). Sometimes we lose sight of our own sin, and where the King of kings has both *brought* us from and *bought* us from.

What happens, for instance, when we try to do what is right, but get berated for it? I know this is sometimes tough to bear, especially because the sports arena can be a lonely road. For example, we hear comments when we turn our eyes from an ungodly magazine, refrain from cursing, or go to chapel or church. But Jesus says He will never leave us nor forsake us. He understands all we go through and cares about every detail of our lives!

The next time you are persecuted for the light that beams forth from your presence—pray! And choose to forgive. You may not feel like forgiving, but our walk with God is not based on feelings. It's based on faith. We forgive because God our Father calls us to forgive. We choose to obey.

Is forgiveness hard for you? Have you been working on developing a Christ-like heart, one that is soft toward those who are caught in sin or who turn against you?

GAME PLAN

So, as you stand shagging fly balls in the outfield during batting practice, pray for those around you. God will soften your heart toward those you struggle with. With a heart like His, forgiveness will be as natural as breathing.

—*Kim Braatz-Voisard, former pro baseball player*

From the Playbook:
Read Genesis 33:1–11.

IMAGINE GREATNESS

*"If anything is excellent or praiseworthy—
think about such things."* PHILIPPIANS 4:8

We think about a lot of things. If we were to transcribe every thought that went through our heads in just one day, the task would be a multi-day project.

Participation in sports gives rise to a whole different set of thoughts from everyday life. During workouts, we may be thinking about how much weight we can lift, how to implement new plays or skills, how hard to push while nursing an injury, or even where the next competitive event will take place.

One skill many athletes use during training and competition is imaging. This is the ability to create mental pictures or imagery that can assist you in becoming more proficient in any area you desire. Some people use imagery to practice a technique without doing the actual movement. Others use imagery to build their confidence as they watch themselves doing what is necessary to win their event. Imagery is not magical nor does it guarantee victory, but it is an effective tool that utilizes the God-given ability to think about things that are excellent.

Imagery is often a vehicle through which athletes imagine greatness—whether they eventually achieve it or not. How gracious it was of God to design a way for us to see the goodness and the excitement of life through our mind's eye! Whether in the heat of competition or resting quietly at home, make a point to think about, as Paul put it, excellent and praiseworthy things. And don't forget, that means we need also to think about the great things God has done for us. Now, that's true greatness!

—*Jean Driscoll, eight-time Boston Marathon wheelchair champion*

GAME PLAN

How can thinking about things that are excellent strengthen your relationship with Jesus Christ? What are some not-so-excellent things that need to be eliminated from your thoughts?

From the Playbook:
Read 2 Samuel 7:1–17.

IT WASN'T MY FAULT!

"The sluggard says, 'There is a lion outside!' "
PROVERBS 22:13

Have you ever noticed how creative some athletes can be? Just listen to them make excuses after an embarrassing mistake: *The court was too slippery. The sun was in my eyes. The fans were against me. I broke a string. I pulled a muscle. The other guy (team) cheated. The ref was blind.*

My all-time favorite comes from the NFL player who said he missed a field goal because—and I quote—"My helmet was too tight. It was squeezing my brain."

And we thought it was because he made a bad kick.

After a while, you find yourself wanting to shout, "Come *on*, guys! Enough with the excuses. Just do your best and play the game!"

Come to think of it, that's pretty good advice for those of us who are "running the race" of faith. It's easy to make excuses when we fall short of the goal. We can think of all kinds of reasons for our failures and mistakes. There's always someone or something we can blame.

But playing the blame game doesn't get us anywhere. Excuses don't fix the problem. They just waste our valuable time and keep us from focusing on the finish line. In Philippians 3:13–14, Paul said, "Forgetting what is behind and straining toward what is ahead, I press on toward the goal to win the prize for which God has called me heavenward in Christ Jesus."

Don't let excuses keep you from moving ahead in the race of life. Stay focused—and run for all you're worth!

—*Christin Ditchfield*

GAME PLAN

Have you been making excuses to cover your mistakes? Ask God for forgiveness instead. He'll help you overcome your failures and give you strength to run the race.

From the Playbook:
Read Colossians 3:12–24.

THE GREAT CHASE

"Come near to God and he will come near to you."
JAMES 4:8

A friend of mine has a one-year-old son named Skyler. He is eager for his independence but still wants Mom close at hand. She has always been his source of food and love, clean diapers, and endless snuggling. Mom is the center of his world, and he is keenly aware of her presence.

I saw this illustrated as I watched Skyler playing on the floor while his mom moved around the room. He would look over frequently to make sure she was nearby, then he'd smile and go on playing. The crisis came when Mom left the room. No more than five seconds had passed when he let out a piercing cry, as if to say, "Hey, you're too far away!" And he took off speed-crawling, chasing her with all his might.

Do you see the comparison to our relationship with God? He takes care of everything His children need, whether it's food on our plates or a trial to teach us patience. We may never realize this side of heaven just how careful He is to ensure that we are being made more like Him.

God our Father wants us to glance at Him constantly, to stay in close contact with Him. And we can be sure that if we don't, it is we who moved, unlike Skyler's mom.

"Come near to God and he will come near to you" (James 4:8). He is our safe place. All through history, He has proved that He is there for His children when they need Him. Our job is to make sure we stay in the same room with Him.

— *Sue Semrau, women's college basketball coach*

GAME PLAN

What is it like to stray from God? Have you done that and found the loneliness and despair? What are some things that keep you from God?

From the Playbook:
Read Psalm 62:1–8.

KEEPING YOUR FOCUS

"Let us fix our eyes on Jesus." HEBREWS 12:2

When standing at the free throw line, preparing to take my foul shot, I have learned one basic principle that brings success. For the split second before I shoot the ball, I must focus my eyes on one particular spot on the rim.

From years of practice, I have trained my eyes to locate this spot, focus on it and then let my body do the rest. When I get lazy in this particular action, I start to let my eyes wander and I begin to see other distractions. I might notice the fans cheering against me or see players moving into position or even notice the team mascot running down the sideline. At this point I know that I have lost my focus.

So it is the same in life. In the book of Hebrews we are told to "Fix our eyes on Jesus . . . " We need to daily remind ourselves who it is we live for and what our ultimate goal is in life.

When we give too much attention to our circumstances and surroundings, we become distracted and lose our focus. Jesus promises to give us strength if we would make Him the center of our life. Just as I must take the time to train my eyes to focus on the hoop, so must I also take the time to get away from the distractions of living and focus my mind and my eyes on the One who brings me victory in life.

—*Leighann Reimer, former pro basketball player*

GAME PLAN

What are the distractions in my life that pull my attention away from Jesus? How can I minimize their influence on my focus time? What can I do to draw my attention to Jesus and keep it there?

From the Playbook:

Read Proverbs 4:25–27; Psalm 25:15; Psalm 141:8.

EMPTY GRANDSTANDS

"The manifestation of the Spirit is given for the common good." 1 CORINTHIANS 12:7

You can play sports without spectators, but you can't play without athletes.

A few years ago, a couple of high schools were having some trouble with basketball fans who refused to behave themselves during and after the contests. So to avoid trouble, the second game of the season between the two schools was played without spectators. The only people allowed in the gym were the players, the refs, the coaches, and the scorekeepers. The only sounds were the bounce of the ball, the players' comments, the shrill sound of the whistle, the blare of the buzzer, and the usual bellowing of the coaches.

It proved that although spectators are an important element, they aren't essential.

Sometimes we get that mixed up. We think our main job is to be a spectator—especially at church. We think we've done something important by showing up and watching the action at church.

Problem is, God never meant His followers to be spectators in the work of the church. He gave talents and skills to His followers—and those gifts are not grandstand tickets to the game of life. They are spiritual abilities to be used on the playing field of school, work, or community.

God's strategy for His work is not like a pro sports team. It does not call for all the work to be done by high-salaried professionals. Rather, every believer has his own position and role on the team. He has appropriate gifts from the Spirit to use for God's glory.

Wouldn't it be great if so many of God's people were involved in the game that the grandstands were empty!

—*Mart DeHaan*

GAME PLAN

If you don't know what your gifts are, set an appointment with your pastor. He'd be glad to help you discover what God has prepared you to do.

From the Playbook:
Read 1 Corinthians 12:1–11.

GOING DOWN TO GO UP

"He will make your paths straight." PROVERBS 3:6

For one young hoopster, the choice was simple. For Erin Buescher, that is. A 6'3" basketball star, she left the University of California at Santa Barbara—after winning three straight Big West Conference Player of the Year awards—for tiny Master's College.

Why would this likely future WNBA first-round draft pick leave the bright lights of NCAA Division I ball for the warm glow of a small NAIA school? It's simple. She wanted to draw closer to God.

Erin says that while she tasted success at Santa Barbara, inside she felt distant from Jesus Christ. "I felt like I had gotten to a place where I wasn't really happy with who I was. I felt dry inside, like a desert. Like nothing spiritual was going on."

So, for her senior year, Erin went to a smaller, Christ-centered school to grow in her knowledge of God. "I have been blown away with what the Lord is doing with me," she said while at Master's College. "I feel like I am changing every day. The Bible and the Lord are coming alive to me like they never had before."

To some, it may appear that Erin took a step down. But her smile and inner peace showed that, for her, things were definitely looking up!

Are you willing to take a "step down" to follow God? If God wants us to pass up that promotion or quit that high-paying career to work with troubled youth or change schools to grow in our relationship with Him, there is only one way to reply.

"Yes, Lord."

Proverbs tells us that if we trust the Lord, He will make our paths straight.

Erin has trusted Him. How ready are we to do the same?

—Tom Felten

GAME PLAN

Write down any possible "callings" you have sensed are coming from God—new directions, work, ventures. Pray and ask God to reveal whether you should proceed in the new way(s) He has revealed. Show your list to a trusted, mature Christian friend and get his or her counsel.

From the Playbook:
Read Proverbs 3.

LET YOUR LIGHT SHINE

"[So] that they may see your good deeds and praise your Father in heaven." MATTHEW 5:16

Though Lauren Dungy has never competed as a professional athlete, she's asked herself, "If I had a chance to be out there, what would I want people to see about me?" As the wife of former NFL head coach Tony Dungy, Lauren has found that people are looking at her. They want to get something from an interview or from an afternoon with her. Lauren knows she is kind of on stage.

"When I'm asked to speak at a school function or speak in a church or other setting, people are curious about me," Lauren says. "They want to hear the inside scoop, and they're looking to me for some type of direction or inspiration. I don't want to be looked at as poised and professional when I'm on stage while behind the scenes people say, 'Oh, she just loses it.' I want my Christian faith to be something that is obvious in all areas of my life—whether I'm in the spotlight or at home with Tony and our four children."

Lauren and Tony want first and foremost to be consistent with their faith. "Our faith is something that's going to go on forever," Lauren says. "It's not a temporary thing. We don't turn it on and off. We love and serve a powerful God, and we look to Him for direction in all aspects of life. The God we serve is One we worship and give glory to every day—not just when we're with other Christians."

We are called to "let our light shine before men" (Matthew 5:16). How are you doing?

—*Roxanne Robbins*

GAME PLAN

Write about a time when you wanted to hide your faith in Christ but didn't. What did you see God do as a result?

From the Playbook:
Read Matthew 5:13–16.

WORK ON THE FUNDAMENTALS

"For the word of God is living and active. Sharper than any double-edged sword, it penetrates even to dividing soul and spirit." HEBREWS 4:12

On the 1980s, I played professional women's basketball for the WBL—the Women's Basketball League. Although this league is no longer in existence, to play professional women's basketball was a dream come true for me. I showed up for the first practice session with the expectation that we would learn some new advanced skills at the professional level. To my amazement, it was quite the opposite. We spent most of the first few months of practice working on the basic fundamentals of basketball.

Now as I go from place to place teaching the skills of basketball, I have noticed that those who are grounded in the fundamental skills of the game play the game at a higher level. When the competition gets tougher, we can rely on the fundamental skills to give us the solid foundation we need. Every skill I demonstrate in my basketball show is based on very fundamental drills.

This is also true in life. I find answers in God's Word for problem areas in my own life. I memorize that Scripture, then when the trial comes again I can defeat the enemy with the Word of God, my solid foundation—my fundamentals. The Bible says in 2 Timothy 3:16, "All Scripture is given by inspiration of God, and is profitable for doctrine, for reproof, for correction, for instruction in righteousness" (NKJV). That's as fundamental as it gets.

—*Tanya Crevier, basketball showperson*

GAME PLAN

What is your basis for life? Is it the truth of God's Word? Write down three essential truths that you will not waver from.

From the Playbook:
Read Psalm 119:91–93.

19

NIGHTMARE AT THE OLYMPICS

"Through all this, Job did not sin nor did he blame God."
JOB 1:22 NASB

On January 31, 2002, US Olympic skier Caroline Lalive wrote in a diary article for the *Denver Post,* "Less than 10 days. The days are passing quickly, and my dream is becoming a reality. The Olympics are . . . what many dream of most of their lives."

When the Olympics came, though, reality turned out to be more of a nightmare than a dream. In the downhill, Caroline likely had a medal-winning run going but crashed in the bottom half. The combined, her strongest event, was next, but again she fell in the slalom portion, putting her 17 seconds (roughly the equivalent of 10 years in skiing) behind the leaders. She still had one more chance in the Super-G. But five gates in she went down again. An Olympic dream—over.

When I interviewed Caroline about a month after the Olympics, she said, "It was tough, and I questioned a lot of things. But you have to have faith that in the long run, God's plan is going to be way better. I just need to keep trusting the Lord and submersing myself in the Word and in prayer so I can continue to draw strength from Him even in some pretty big turmoil."

Have you experienced a major disappointment recently? Don't neglect spending regular time reading the Bible and praying. Caroline found help reading the Old Testament book of Job. "He must really have wondered what was going on too!" she observed. You may find help there as well.

—*Brian Hettinga*

GAME PLAN

Make it a point to reach out to someone you know who has experienced a serious setback recently. Sincerely ask how he or she is doing and really listen. If you get the chance, let your friend know how God's Word has encouraged you during a disappointing time.

From the Playbook:
Read Job 1.

JOY IN THE JOURNEY

"God intended it for good." GENESIS 50:20

World-class cyclist Jacqui Lockwood says her life was changed forever in February 1997. That's when doctors discovered a grapefruit-size tumor on her heart. The diagnosis: non-Hodgkins lymphoma. As Lockwood tells it, she went from "world-class to couch-class in one week's time!" She faced months of chemotherapy and an uncertain future. It should have been devastating. But it wasn't.

"The more often I talk about it and look back on it, the more I realize how special it was," says Jacqui.

Special?

"I just had a real peace about it, that for some reason it was something I needed to go through," Jacqui explains. She was overwhelmed by the prayer support and encouragement she received from her church family and the members of her Bible-study group. Even her son's classmates and their families gathered for prayer on Jacqui's behalf. Having been a Christian for just a short time, this outpouring of love and concern was a new experience for her.

"It was also a wonderful witnessing opportunity," Lockwood says. As she underwent chemotherapy, Jacqui freely shared her faith with the other patients who were "facing death head-on."

Jacqui's experience with cancer led her to re-evaluate her priorities, especially in regard to her sport. "I learned that God gives, and He can take away. On the big tandem of life, God's the captain—I'm just the stoker! Now, whenever I race, I do it for His glory."

Her bout with cancer could have been a tragic experience. But Jacqui chose to trust God—for good or for bad. She found joy in a journey that brought her to a deeper relationship with Him.

—*Christin Ditchfield*

GAME PLAN

Take a few moments to think about the tough times you've experienced in your own life. Write down what you've learned and how you've grown through those times.

From the Playbook:
Read James 1:2–4, 12.

JESUS AND THE WOMAN

*"There is neither . . . male nor female. For you are
all one in Christ."* GALATIANS 3:28

Women athletes have always faced challenges when pursuing athletic goals. Many challenges have been brought on by a lack of opportunity, by clear opposition, and by an ignorance of their abilities. As a child, I was initially discouraged from pursuing my athletic dreams because of comparison to my male counterparts and because of appearances. Fortunately, things were beginning to change, and eventually women's sports were encouraged and the opportunities became limitless.

Can you think of anyone in your sphere of influence who is somehow looked down on by others? What can you do to make that person feel the love of Christ as the Savior did for the woman at the well?

Women during the time of Jesus faced some negative attitudes as well. Women were viewed as lesser citizens and often treated with contempt and disrespect. How uncomfortable and shocking it must have been for the men in Jesus' day, then, when He lifted women from the agony of degradation and servitude to the joy of fellowship with Him.

This is clearly demonstrated by the act of love He showed to the woman at the well. Being a Samaritan was enough to make her despised by the Jews, but being a woman further diminished her worth. Praise God that our loving Savior shared with her the spiritual water that would forever quench her thirst! He led her to the one true God—regardless of the barriers presented by society.

We must strive to do the same with people in our sphere of influence. Are you willing to come out of your comfort zone and make a difference in someone's life—especially someone society does not consider valuable?

—*LaVonna Martin-Floreal, Olympic silver medalist, track*

From the Playbook:
Read the entire story of the Samaritan woman in John 4:1–26.

NOT MY PLANS, BUT HIS

"Now to him who is able to do immeasurably more than all we ask or imagine." EPHESIANS 3:20

A major fear for most athletes is injury. It is crucial for our bodies to be healthy. In February 2003, I faced this fear head on when I severely injured my ankle during a game. After sitting out for several weeks, followed by an unsuccessful attempt at returning to play, I was eventually sent for an MRI. The results were startling. A severely bruised ankle-bone, a small bone chip, and several other old injuries had combined to produce the extreme pain I was experiencing. The recommended solution was major surgery.

This was not in my plans. In two months I was to compete in the Pan American Games, in three months the Olympic qualifications, and I was in the middle of signing my third professional contract. I had no time for surgery and six months of rehabilitation.

Thankfully, God had something else planned. From the day I injured my ankle I prayed that God would heal me. I didn't know God's will for this specific situation, but I rested in the promise that He is able to do immeasurably more than I could ask or imagine. I waited on Him, and although there was no spontaneous, dramatic healing, God definitely answered my prayer.

Despite the doctor's prognosis, I played in both competitions, and to this day I am able to play pain-free. No surgery was needed, because I had the best doctor of all—a heavenly Healer.

When we think things are impossible, that is when God takes over.

— *Leighann Reimer, former pro basketball player*

GAME PLAN

What situation do you face today that is beyond your control? Is there anything holding you back from giving it to God in faith—trusting that whichever way He handles your situation, it is best. What can you do while you wait on His answer?

From the Playbook:
Read James 5:13–18.

BEARING YOUR CROSS

"If anyone would come after me, he must . . . take up his cross and follow me." MATTHEW 16:24

As Christians, many times we are called upon to bear our cross; to endure pain and suffering in the midst of our circumstances.

Just because we try to live according to the Spirit and not according to the flesh (Galatians 5:16–26), we are sometimes talked about, ridiculed, judged, lied about, misunderstood, and a host of other discouraging things. It is during these times that we might feel the desire to abandon God's will and begin implementing our own will. We feel "the cross" is too difficult to bear (1 Corinthians 10:13).

We grow weary in doing good things, we stop listening to the Holy Spirit, and we begin listening to our own flesh. The Spirit says, "Endure," but the flesh says, "Walk away! You don't have to take this."

The Spirit says, "Be patient," but the flesh says, "I want it now." The Spirit says, "Think of those who need to hear My Word," but the flesh says, "Think of yourself."

The Spirit and our flesh are in constant battle for control of our life (Galatians 5:17–18), and if we are not connected to God through fellowship in the Spirit, we allow our flesh to lead us away from God (John 15:6).

It is through you that some may come to know Christ. As you are called to "bear your cross," put God before self, and allow Him to use you as a vessel to lead as many people as possible to Jesus.

—*Kedra Holland-Corn, former WNBA player*

GAME PLAN

What is my response to the idea of bearing a cross? What did Jesus mean when He spoke the words of Matthew 16:24?

From the Playbook:

Read Matthew 16:24–28 and Mark 14:32–42.

24

LOVE, TOMMY, AND JESUS

"There is no fear in love. But perfect love drives out fear."
1 JOHN 4:18

I met Tommy Amico at a softball tournament in July 1997. Right away I liked the qualities I saw in him. But Tommy lived in South Carolina, and I lived in Arizona. So, at the beginning, we started a friendship on the phone. Through our conversations, I was able to share God's plan of salvation with him. After attending an Athletes In Action meeting at the University of South Carolina, he met with an AIA staff member, and Tommy trusted Christ as Savior.

Through my relationship with Tommy, God has showed me that all things are possible if we allow Him to lead us and if it is according to His will. After seeing each other for less than two months total, Tommy and I were married in January 1999. On our wedding day, I felt the love that the Bible speaks about, but I have also learned through marriage that it takes work and a daily commitment to love each other.

I love my husband very much, but if I want to talk about love in the greatest sense, I have to talk about God.

God's love is the greatest. For instance, with God in our lives, we never have to worry about earning His love—or most important, losing His love. God is the true giver of unconditional love.

John tells us "God is love. Whoever lives in love lives in God, and God in him . . . There is no fear in love. But perfect love drives out fear" (1 John 4:16, 18).

When I talk to people who are longing for the perfect relationship, I don't talk about Tommy and me, as happy as we are. I tell them that I know Someone who will never let them down and will never stop loving them. That person is Jesus Christ, and He's waiting for us with open arms.

—*Leah O'Brien-Amico, Olympic gold medalist, softball*

GAME PLAN

Have you experienced God's love through Jesus Christ? If not, trust Jesus today.

From the Playbook:

Read 1 John 4.

PUTTING FIRST THINGS FIRST

"Seek first his kingdom and his righteousness, and all these things will be given to you." MATTHEW 6:33

I learned the importance of putting God first in my life fairly early in my spiritual journey.

During my senior year at the University of South Carolina, my focus in life started turning to "me." I had finished my junior year as a first-team All-American and SEC Player of the Year in golf, and I was looking forward to my senior year as being just as successful. I had big plans, and I thought I had everything mapped out for a successful year. Unfortunately, as I got more absorbed in all the things I needed to get accomplished, I forgot about the importance of keeping my daily time with the Lord.

As my senior year wore on, I completely neglected my quiet times with God, and I became discontented with my life. It wasn't that I totally forgot about God or denied being a Christian. I still went to church and hung around Christian friends. What I didn't do was spend the necessary one-on-one time with God to keep my focus on what God wanted me to do.

I was fortunate, however, to have close friends to remind me about keeping God first. After shifting my focus back to God, the things of life became less significant in the bigger frame of things. With my perspectives back in order, I was able to finish my senior year with the right mindset and place sixth in the NCAA Division I national championships.

It is not that God doesn't want us to set high goals or become successful; He does. But first, He wants to be involved with our lives, and He wants us to include Him in our successes—then He can rightfully get the glory.

—*Siew-Ai Lim, former LPGA golfer*

GAME PLAN

What has been sneaking its way to No. 1 in your life, shoving your relationship with God down the list? What can you do today and this week to make sure things get put back in place?

From the Playbook:
Read Numbers 18:8–29.

MEETING MICHAEL

"But when he, the Spirit of truth, comes, he will guide you into all truth." JOHN 16:13

Several years ago, I met Michael Jordan through a prison ministry. At the time, he was a college student, and he was a guest speaker at the event.

A few years later, I was the half-time entertainment for the Chicago Bulls, and I chatted with Michael briefly several times. He would share a few personal things with me because I had known him when he was a college student, and he asked me if I was still involved with the prison ministry. That was special. I realized he still knew who I was. He knew me.

Fans love to know important things about their favorite athletes. When they do that, they know about them, but they don't necessarily know them like I know Michael. That was much more meaningful than just knowing about him.

On a grander scale, for 23 years of my life as a faithful church attender, I knew all about God and what Jesus had done on the cross. I knew the facts about Jesus, but I didn't know Him on a personal level. Until I trusted Him as Savior, I just knew about Him. I didn't know that once His Holy Spirit came to dwell in my own heart He would guide me in such a personal way. The Bible says in John 16:13 that the Spirit will guide you into all truth.

Now that I know Jesus, I no longer wait for a chance to see Him at a church meeting like I used to. Jesus lives inside me in the person of His Holy Spirit. I have a relationship with Him on a personal level every day of my life.

What a difference there is between knowing Jesus and knowing about Him!

—*Tanya Crevier, basketball showperson*

GAME PLAN

Think seriously about this question: Do you know Jesus in a personal way? Have you trusted Him as Savior?

From the Playbook:
Read John 3.

THANKS FOR THE FREE GIFT

"For it is by grace you have been saved, through faith."
EPHESIANS 2:8, 9

Because of the nature of sports, athletes are put under a spotlight. They perform for an audience, and they provide entertainment for society. This is what entices many to become the best at their sport. Those people want to reach stardom, and fame becomes the goal.

I by no means reached stardom in my basketball career at the University of California at Santa Barbara, but playing at the college level on a successful basketball team gave me some mild glimpses of what that success entails. Sure, it was fun to some degree, but it was also very empty. As long as we were winning and playing well, many loved us. However, as soon as we played below expectations or began losing, all our "friends" were nowhere to be found. There was a clear message to be learned: Performance is everything. In order to be liked, we had to perform well; otherwise, the stands would be empty.

It is because of this lesson that I am so acutely aware of God and His unconditional love for me. He couldn't care less if I play well or if we win the ballgame. His love for me is not based on works but on the fact that I am His child through faith in Jesus Christ. I have not done anything to receive it; it is His free gift to me, undeserved and unearned.

As a child of God I want to make my relationship with Him the No. 1 priority in my life. That's why I strive to play for an audience of one, to be aware of His presence at all times, and to desire His love and adoration only. I hope that is your goal as well.

—*Erin Buescher Perperoglu, former WNBA guard*

GAME PLAN

What is the No. 1 priority in your life? If it is your relationship with God, how do you demonstrate it—not to others, but to God?

From the Playbook:

Read Ephesians 2.

AN ATHLETE ANSWERS THE CALL

"Abraham . . . was strengthened in his faith and gave glory to God." ROMANS 4:18–20

Catriona LeMay Doan. You say those three words in Canada, and you are sure to bring a smile to any sports fan. Catriona has wowed Canadians with her Olympic gold-medal performances in speed skating.

Interestingly, it was at the Olympics that she first realized she needed to be saved. Here's how it happened.

After the 1994 Olympics In Lillehammer, Norway, she saw a simple sign with the words "Athletes In Action" and a phone number. "I don't know now why I called," Catriona says with a laugh. "I guess I thought, 'I'm an athlete,' and I thought it applied to me."

Soon afterward, Catriona met with AIA staff person Harold Cooper, a friendly, fatherly man who has since become her spiritual mentor.

"Harold went through the gospel with me, but it was sort of too much all at once," Doan remembers. "He asked me if I wanted to become a Christian, and I was like, 'Well, maybe I will talk this over with [her husband] Bart first,' I was trying to postpone it. A few weeks later, though, I decided that it was the choice I wanted to make."

Since she gave her life to Christ in the summer of 1994, Catriona has established herself as the world's top female sprinter. In all her personal victories and defeats she tries to integrate her faith with her emotions.

"My faith is a comfort, and it gives me a different reason to be doing the sport."

How does your faith give you strength? There can be no better source of power and might than to have a heart sold out to God.

—*Lorilee Craker*

GAME PLAN

Since I came to faith in Christ, what remarkable things have I done that I know I wouldn't have done without God's help? Make a list of five ways your faith helps you in your everyday life.

From the Playbook:
Read Romans 4.

THE ENCOURAGER

"Consider it pure joy, my brothers, whenever you face trials of many kinds." JAMES 1:2–4

I had one of the most disappointing years of my career in 2003. I had made four cuts in 14 tournaments, and for the first time in my golf career, I was in the red financially.

Times like that make me question if I need to stay the course as an LPGA player. I wondered if all the hard work I had done over the years was really working, or if I had just hit my peak. Thoughts of giving up were there.

Fortunately for me, I had a tremendous coach who continued to encourage me to keep persevering. He saw my potential and knew that I had so much more inside of me to become one of the top players on Tour. His encouragement and my continued perseverance in working on my game paid off as I had one of my most successful seasons on the LPGA Tour in 2004.

Looking back, I see how that parallels with my spiritual life. There are times when I feel like I'm getting nowhere in my spiritual journey, and I feel beaten down. I wonder if the difficulties I face in life are worth the effort I'm putting in as a Christian and a follower of Christ.

When we feel that way, the good news is that all of us as followers of Christ have an Encourager, the Holy Spirit. He's the still, quiet voice that tells us to keep going. He's the one who says we have so much more to achieve if only we stay the course. Listen to the Encourager. Persevere and keep pressing on to the finish line.

—*Siew-Ai Lim, former LPGA golfer*

GAME PLAN

What is discouraging me right now? How much time have I spent talking to the Lord about it—and then listening to the Holy Spirit's encouraging guidance?

From the Playbook:

Memorize Romans 15:13.

FINDING TRUE FULFILLMENT

"I consider everything a loss compared to . . . knowing Christ."
PHILIPPIANS 3:8

Many professional athletes look like they have everything—money, popularity, excitement, and security. What I've noticed through several years of observing athletes up close is that they often experience deep internal struggles. Loneliness creeps in when they spend countless nights on the road. And they face a tremendous amount of pressure to perform day after day.

Olympic silver medalist Rosalynn Sumners realizes how fortunate she was, as a figure skater, to turn pro and make a living with skating following her amateur career. But even in the midst of the glamour, she had times when she longed for circumstances to be different. Rosalynn found that money and fame didn't give her the security and sense of purpose she longed for. She found that hard to explain, even to her closest friends, because people didn't feel sorry for her when they realized how much money she made as a pro. Rosalynn didn't want sympathy, though. She simply wanted to meet the needs that go deeper than her Olympic experiences and her career—the basic needs we all have.

Several years ago she found what was missing—a personal relationship with Jesus Christ. At that point she asked the Lord to take the reins of her life. Rosalynn found that Jesus Christ is the only person she can be completely vulnerable and raw and honest with.

God alone provides ultimate fulfillment. Although you will always wrestle with various trials and times of loneliness in life, if you have put your trust in Jesus Christ, you have a friend who is with you no matter what your situation. He alone can give true fulfillment.

—*Roxanne Robbins*

GAME PLAN

Do you consider everything else a loss compared to knowing Christ? What does this question mean to you? Think deeply about this and ask God to show you what you might be clinging to for fulfillment instead of Him.

From the Playbook:
Read Philippians 3:1–14.

TOUGH STUFF

"Be joyful in hope, patient in affliction, faithful in prayer."
ROMANS 12:12

Playing NCAA Division I athletics is never a walk in the park. And when you play for a perennial power, it's downright tough. There's the constant pressure to win. There's the conflict between school and sports. There's the excessive attention you get from fans and the media.

When you throw an injury into all of this, it can become one maniacal mix. That's what happened to Jenny Evans, who starred as an outside hitter for the women's volleyball team at UCLA in the early 1990s.

She was forced to sit out a season with a painful right shoulder injury. During that time some of their opponents accused her of "wimping out." They implied that her year off was unnecessary—that she left her team when her abilities were sorely needed.

Just a year before, Jenny had been a *Volleyball Monthly* All-American, Volleyball Coaches Association second-team All-American, and member of the All-NCAA Tournament team.

But Jenny persevered through the injury. She came back to help UCLA have another banner season. "A lot of my drive came from knowing that God was [allowing] this trial," she said, "and I needed to please Him by being strong."

She was prepared for the tough stuff because she knew God would use it for her good. Jenny's life illustrates that "suffering produces perseverance; perseverance, character; and character, hope" (Romans 5:3-4).

Jenny said, "I was hoping . . . that through my play, people could see that God is No. 1 in my life." It's evident that people can also see Christ through her as one who is "patient in affliction."

Are you living like that?

—*Tom Felten*

> **GAME PLAN**
>
> Write down the three toughest things you've had to endure in the past week. Next to each write down one way you can bless others through those tough things.

From the Playbook:
Read Romans 5:1-11.

GIVE IT TO GOD!

"Cast all your anxiety on him because he cares for you."
1 PETER 5:7

Mary Lou Retton is happily married and living in Houston, Texas, with her husband, Shannon Kelley, and their children.

Mary Lou's fame and her personality as an Olympic champion gymnast in the 1988 Summer Games have made her a popular conference speaker and a sought-after spokesperson for a wide variety of corporations, organizations, and causes. For a number of years, she's been on the speaker's circuit, talking about winning and her Olympic experiences.

But recently, she's found herself speaking out about something much more personal. "I'm a Christian," Retton says. "I believe in Jesus Christ, who died on the cross for my sins."

Lately, Mary Lou says she's been learning about patience. "There are things I've been working on for years, asking God for His guidance and direction. But it doesn't work on my timeline; it works on the Lord's timeline. That's been very frustrating to me! I'm trying to accept that sometimes my prayers are answered 'No.' Sometimes when the Lord doesn't give me something or answer my prayer right away, He's protecting me. I may not be ready for a certain thing at this point in my life. I just have to be patient and totally trust Him."

Retton has a piece of paper taped to her desk that reads: "Good morning! This is God. I will be handling all of your problems today. I will not need your help. So, have a good day!"

"Isn't that great!" exclaims Retton. "I love it! That's what I try to live my day by, not stressing over the little things, the things that are out of our control. 'Cause we can worry ourselves sick—and worry is such a sin! Just give it to God!"

—*Christin Ditchfield*

> **GAME PLAN**
>
> What three burdens have you been carrying around for the past couple of days? Write them on a piece of paper, pray for God to take them, and then throw the paper away.

From the Playbook:
Read Psalm 55.

JULIE'S JOY

"Your joy in Christ Jesus will overflow on account of me."
PHILIPPIANS 1:26

On her freshman year at the University of Arizona, Felicity Willis began a friendship that would change her life. That's when she met softball teammate Julie Reitan. Right away, Felicity noticed something different about Julie.

"She was so happy all the time! She always had a smile on her face," recalls Felicity. "She would do just about anything for anybody."

The two teammates quickly became close friends.

But later that same year, an unspeakable tragedy struck. Julie Reitan died suddenly of complications from diabetes. Felicity was devastated. In her grief, she found herself asking a lot of questions about life and death—and her friend's faith.

GAME PLAN

Do your friends know you for a joy that they can trace back to Jesus?

"I came to realize that the reason Julie was so filled with life and so filled with joy was because of her relationship with God. I decided that was what I wanted—a personal relationship with Jesus Christ."

Willis began attending campus Bible studies and sports camps organized by Athletes In Action. It helped her get a handle on her newfound faith. Felicity says her life was changed forever by the lessons she learned from their special friendship.

"I don't take life for granted anymore, because it can be taken away from you just like that. I have an inner peace knowing that when I do die, I'll go to heaven. Now I'm just trying to live my life the way God wants me to."

Julie's joy was a testimony in life, and it was what convinced Felicity in death. As believers, do we have a convincing joy?

—*Christin Ditchfield*

From the Playbook:
Read Philippians 1.

NEW SEASON, NEW GOALS

"The Spirit intercedes for the saints in accordance with God's will." ROMANS 8:27

One of the great things about sports is that you get to start over each season.

You and everyone else begin the season exactly the same. No matter how well or poorly you played last season, when that first ball gets teed up in the first tournament of the season, everybody is at zero.

When I begin a new golf season on the LPGA Tour, I have two goals in mind as I look at my schedule and plan my year. I want to set goals that continue to push my talent forward, but I also want to keep in rhythm with the goals and direction that God has planned for me.

At the beginning of each calendar year, I sit down and pray about what God wants to accomplish through me. In the back of my mind I have evaluated the previous year's goals, which I placed before God last year. I like to set challenging goals, but in accordance with God's will for my life. If my goals are pleasing to Him, then the Holy Spirit inside of me will allow me to feel good about my direction for each new year. I have to be comfortable with my goals on the inside before I can attain anything on the outside.

Then I can turn my goals over to God, depending on Him to guide me throughout the season—no matter what happens.

Think about the goals you set—whether it's for school, work, or family. Do you make sure to include God in your plans?

—*Wendy Ward, LPGA golfer*

GAME PLAN

What were your goals at the start of this year? Is it time for a mid-year review? What can you set as goals that you and God can work on for the rest of the year?

From the Playbook:

Read about Jesus and His desire to do God's will in John 6:38–40.

WHICH WAY DO I GO?

"Your ears will hear a voice behind you." ISAIAH **30:21**

Before she was even 18, Krissy Wendell had been called the best female ice hockey player in the country. As a high school senior, Wendell scored an astonishing 166 points (110 goals and 56 assists) in 27 games. Her phenomenal success led her to a crisis of sorts when she was invited to play on the US National Women's Team.

"I really struggled with whether or not I should go to college or go out and train with the US Team for the Olympics," she recalls. "I've never spent so much time praying and trying to figure out the right decision. I kept going back and forth: 'Go to college; Don't go to college.' Ultimately my parents said, 'You need to keep praying about it and figure out what God wants you to do. When you decide, you'll know it's right because you'll have peace about it.'

Write down four or five decisions you need to make in the next few weeks. Pray about each one specifically, and jot down any thoughts or direction you receive over time.

"One of my favorite Bible verses is Psalm 37:4: 'Delight yourself in the Lord and he will give you the desires of your heart.' I knew I could trust God to lead me in the right path. And there's no time limit on prayer. If you pray long enough, you'll know where God is leading you."

In the end, Wendell decided to join the National Team, preparing for the 2002 Olympics. She describes the 2-year training period as a thrilling experience—the opportunity of a lifetime.

Like Krissy, we all have to make important decisions that will have a great impact on our future. God promises to give us His wisdom in every circumstance. But we have to ask!

—*Christin Ditchfield*

From the Playbook:
Read James 1:5 and Daniel 2:20–22.

TRAINING AND THINKING

"Finally, brothers, whatever is true, . . . if anything is excellent or praiseworthy—think about such things." PHILIPPIANS 4:8

Training 25 hours a week to compete in the triathlon, I put in many miles looking at a black line on the bottom of the pool, pedaling my bike on the roads, or running trails.

I could just fritter away this time, letting my mind wander to things of this world. Or, as the verse today says, I could think about whatever is excellent and praiseworthy—all things from God.

One way to think about such things is to sing songs in your head. If you are like me, sometimes I get a song stuck in my head, and I can't get it out. Instead of this song being some catchy Top 40 tune that I just heard at the grocery store (and know only one line to!), I've taken a proactive approach to this "song in my head" problem.

I've written down the names or key phrases of my favorite songs that we sing in church or that I hear on the Christian radio station. I've taped this list to the handlebar stem of my bike and written another list under the bill of my running hat. Now like a CD changer, while training I can proactively select from my list songs that inspire me. When I ride or run up hills, I sing songs of God's power. On other days when I'm pedaling through beautiful mountains and I become overwhelmed by His incredible creation, I sing songs of praise.

GAME PLAN

How can you begin to program your mind with thoughts that are excellent and praiseworthy? Can a switch to Christian music do that? How much of your time do you think God-directed thoughts?

What a difference it makes to think about God's power, love, and grace through song, rather than having songs dealing with things of this world floating through my head.

—*Barb Lindquist, Olympic triathlete*

From the Playbook:
Read Psalm 108.

ROCK SOLID

"My hope comes from [God]. He alone is my rock and my salvation." Psalm 62:5–8

Playing basketball at Boston College was an incredible experience for me. Our program went from not even making the NCAA tournament my freshman year to making it to the Sweet Sixteen for the first time in school history my junior year.

Finally, it was my senior year, a year during which I was challenged to lead our young team to more success. We had just finished a remarkable regular season, and the intensity was building as I realized that the next few games would be my last ever in college.

Our team was headed for the Big East tournament in Hartford, Connecticut, where 16,000 fans would be cheering on the UConn Huskies, the dominating team in the Big East Conference.

I was nervous. All I wanted in my college career was to win the Big East tournament—to be the best in the conference. It was here that I called upon the Lord to give me the strength and confidence that I needed throughout this tournament. In Him alone I felt as if I could overcome anything. With that strength, I led our team to win four games in four days, including beating UConn.

God used His words to give me assurance that I could rely on Him as my rock, strength, fortress, and refuge. He would remain stable, and He would not be shaken; therefore, I felt I could not be shaken. I went into the Big East tournament thinking there was no one or no team that could stop me and my team from doing something extraordinary—and that was to win the tournament.

When you are not feeling confident or you are a little nervous or you need an extra boost—seek God. You will find assurance in Him, as He is our steady rock. You may not win the big game, but you know that God will give you strength for any challenge.

—*Amber Jacobs, former WNBA guard*

GAME PLAN

What is coming up in your life that looks as insurmountable as the UConn Huskies? How are you preparing to lean on God's strength?

From the Playbook:

Read Psalm 62.

DO YOU HAVE THE SEAL?

"Having believed, you were marked in him with a seal, the promised Holy Spirit." EPHESIANS 1:13

It's Tuesday and I'm driving to the golf course for my practice round. As I drive through the front gate, I hold up my money clip. The security guard waves and allows me to pass.

The LPGA Tour money clip is a powerful piece of metal. It has my name inscribed on it, along with these words: Ladies Professional Golf Tour. It signifies that I am a member of the Tour, and it enables me access to anywhere I wish around the tournament site. When I wear my money clip, I receive both respect and a right of passage. It's my seal of approval stating that I am a professional golfer.

Unlike the money clip that I had to earn, I have another seal of approval that I experience in my life. This one I got because of nothing I did. When I accepted and trusted Jesus Christ as my personal Savior, God sealed me with His Holy Spirit. This seal gives me full and direct access to God, His promises, and His power.

God tells us in Ephesians 1:14 that the Holy Spirit "is a deposit guaranteeing our inheritance until the redemption of those who are God's possession—to the praise of his glory." For those of us who have trusted Jesus Christ, the seal of the Holy Spirit signifies that we are one of God's children.

Do you have that "seal"? Is the Holy Spirit your guarantee? Don't go anywhere unless you have it!

—*Tracy Hanson, former LPGA golfer*

> **GAME PLAN**
>
> Please make sure you are sealed with God's Holy Spirit. If you've never asked Jesus Christ into your life to forgive you and to save you, do so now. God will mark you "with a seal, the promised Holy Spirit" (Ephesians 1:13).

From the Playbook:

Read these passages about the Holy Spirit:
Ephesians 1:12–14; 2:18, 22; 4:3–4; 6:17–18.

A MUCH BETTER PLAN

"We know that in all things God works for the good of those who love him, who have been called according to his purpose." ROMANS 8:28

It was March 1996, and the American Basketball League announced it was going to start its inaugural season in October. I was in my senior year at Boise State University, and I wanted to turn my dream into reality. I was going to try out.

So when my senior year ended, I went to work on my game. I was practicing so much that I actually began to dream about my shot! I practiced with the BSU players as tryouts grew closer. One day, about halfway into a practice, I made a cut up the court and felt a "snap" in the back of my knee. I hobbled off the court and went straight to the team doctor.

He X-rayed my knee and found a bone spur. The snap I felt was actually my hamstring catching on the spur. The doctor ordered an MRI on my other knee (which had tendonitis), figuring it was a good idea to have both checked at the same time.

The tests showed that my tendon was so badly degenerated the tendon was pulling away from the bone. The doctor said that he needed to do surgery. That would mean a six-month recovery—preventing me from trying out for the ABL.

Although God's Word is extremely comforting, it doesn't always negate the depression one feels when an amazing opportunity has just been missed. That's why it's important to have a relationship with the Lord, to tell Him how you feel and to lean on Him for support. It was during that confusing time that I needed Him more than ever. I was angry, confused, and devastated. I prayed and begged for understanding.

Little did I know that the ABL would fold in a few years and that the WNBA would be the lasting league. But God knew. I believe it is because of His perfect timing, rather than mine, that I became a member of the WNBA.

—*Tricia Binford, former WNBA guard*

GAME PLAN

What situation recently has caused you to wonder where God is? Have you considered that God is looking at the long view of your life and has even this under His control?

From the Playbook:

Read Proverbs 2:3–5.

WHO ARE YOU PLAYING FOR?

"Do it all for the glory of God." 1 CORINTHIANS 10:31

As a freshman, Becky Varnum led her high school tennis team to the Colorado state championships, capturing the singles title herself. This impressive accomplishment brought great expectations with it.

"Everyone started saying, 'You can do it four years in a row!' It put a lot of pressure on me," Varnum recalls. "It was hard to look that far into the future. I tried to just take it one match at a time."

The strategy worked. One match at a time, she captured four consecutive state championships. She graduated with a phenomenal record of 68-0. She never even lost a set!

But the pressure only increased. On the national junior tennis circuit, the competition was more intense. Varnum tasted defeat regularly. She worried that her ranking wasn't good enough for a college scholarship. She was afraid of letting her friends and family down.

After one especially disappointing loss, Becky's mom asked her a question: "Who are you playing for?"

Becky answered, "Well, I'm playing for my coach, because he's put a lot of time into me, and I'm playing for myself, because I need to go to college, and . . ."

Mom interrupted: "You need to be playing for the glory of God!"

Becky's mom reminded her of this simple truth: All God asks is that we do our best for Him—and leave the results in His hands. This truth brought peace and strength to Becky. It can do the same for you!

—*Christin Ditchfield*

> **GAME PLAN**
>
> Who are you playing for? What motivates you today? Ask God to help you do everything for His glory, and trust Him with the outcome.

From the Playbook:

Read Philippians 2:1–11 and Colossians 3:16–17.

STEPPING DOWN TO STEP UP

"Trust in the Lord with all your heart and lean not on your own understanding." PROVERBS 3:5

After high school, I went to the University of California at Santa Barbara on a basketball scholarship. I discovered that playing Division I hoops is similar to working a full-time job. The joy I had once experienced through basketball was soon gone. Worse than that, my relationship with the Lord slowly deteriorated, draining the joy from my life.

The success our team was experiencing was far from gratifying. We were ranked in the Top 10 in the country, we won three consecutive conference titles, and I was named Most Valuable Player of the league three times. But I never felt emptier. Things looked good on the outside, but on the inside I was dying. I knew I wouldn't be able to last much longer. I knew I needed a change.

I was familiar with a small Christian college near LA, and through my mom's prompting, I decided to check it out. I made the call, and within three days I was on the campus of The Master's College, checking into my dorm. The Lord wanted me to take the first step, and when I did, He opened the floodgates. I left my huge Division I university for a small 1,000-person, Christian college in the NAIA.

Many people thought I had thrown away my chance to play in the WNBA. But when the draft came, I ended up with the Minnesota Lynx.

God wants us to trust Him. Sometimes we have to make choices that aren't popular in the world's eyes, but if we are seeking to please God, He will take care of us and provide what He knows we need. It's hard to take that first step when certainty is not guaranteed, but doing so forces us to turn to Him and trust that He is over all.

—*Erin Buescher Perperoglu, former WNBA guard*

GAME PLAN

What are two areas in which you are finding it hard to trust God? What can help you to make that leap to trust Him?

From the Playbook:
Read Proverbs 3.

PRIORITY CHECK

"Seek first his kingdom and his righteousness." MATTHEW 6:33

Can a person who is truly dedicated to a sport keep other priorities straight? After all, someone who is pursuing excellence has so many things to think about.

There's training, which takes careful preparation and immense dedication. And there are affiliations—either with a team or with sponsors, coaches, trainers, and others. There's travel to practices and competitions. There's time that must be spent working on equipment, doing interviews, and pumping iron.

Consider the training regimen Barb Lindquist endured as one of the top triathletes in the United States. In a recent year, she was the Triathlete of the Year. She must have a one-track mind.

Or not. Listen to what she says about her priorities.

"My relationship with Jesus permeates everything," says Barb. "It's who I am. It's in every part of my life, because it is my life."

"I feel [triathlon] is my mission field," says Barb. "I get to spread God's Word to other athletes, to the media, and to people around the world.

"My first priority is my relationship with Jesus. My second priority is my relationship with my husband, Loren, and my third priority is my job, or the triathlon. Even though the triathlon is my third priority, that doesn't mean I won't be the best triathlete I can be. But I also know that if my first two priorities aren't in line, I'll never be the best triathlete I can be."

How we list our priorities tells how we view God's place in our lives. We need a priority check. We need to think it through and make sure the right Person is No. 1.

—*Rob Bentz*

> **GAME PLAN**
>
> This isn't easy, but list the five most important things in your life. Don't try to be super spiritual, but be honest with yourself. Now write down how that list should look.

From the Playbook:
Read: Matthew 22:37–39.

CHOOSE YOUR FRIENDS WISELY

"Walk with the wise." PROVERBS 13:20

When golfer Tracy Hanson was on the LPGA Tour, she chose to spend the majority of her time with people who encourage her to stay true to her Christian beliefs. She avoids close friendships with people who tempt her to do things she knows are wrong.

College friends and her friends on the LPGA Tour have walked with Tracy through the hard and fun times in life. But most important, they have helped her grow in her Christian faith. Tracy's faith has taught her that her worth is from Jesus Christ—and only Him—not from how she performs on the golf course.

"Recognizing Jesus Christ as the source of my true value has helped stabilize my emotions and has given me a bigger perspective of what life is all about," Tracy says. "It's not just about golf and what I do on the golf course. It's about relating with Christ and with people."

"Fortunately, on Tour I'm able to get together with other Christian women. We meet weekly for Bible study, fellowship, and prayer. I am grateful for these relationships and for older mentors who show how to stay strong in the Lord and to experience His grace and comfort in good and difficult times."

Tracy knows that "He who walks with the wise grows wise, but a companion of fools suffers harm" (Proverbs 13:20). Tracy looks to God for wisdom to know whom she should spend time with.

What a great example! We each need to recognize the impact other people have on our choices and the way we view ourselves. That will help us choose friends who lead us closer to God, not farther from Him.

—*Roxanne Robbins*

GAME PLAN

What kind of messages do your friends send you about your value to God? Today, thank a friend or mentor who has helped you better understand God's deep love for you.

From the Playbook:
Read Titus 2:1–8.

44

THE DISEASE OF ME

"The Lord detests all the proud of heart." PROVERBS 16:5

Pat Riley, writing in his book *The Winner Within*, tells about the 1980 World Champion Los Angeles Lakers. After winning the NBA Finals that year, they were recognized as the best basketball team in the world.

Within weeks of their opening game of the next season, Magic Johnson tore cartilage in his knee and was out for three months. The remaining players played their hearts out and were winning 70 percent of their games without Magic but were ignored by the press until the return of their star guard. The players were so resentful that eventually the morale of the entire team collapsed, the guys turned on each other, the coach was fired, and they lost their opening game of the playoffs. Riley said, "Because of greed, pettiness, and resentment, we executed one the fastest falls from grace in NBA history. It was the 'Disease of Me.'"

Whether you are an athlete or not, the vice of pride is the ground in which all other sins grow. It can weasel its way into our lives and destroy relationships and communities. C. S. Lewis said, "Pride is essentially competitive—is competitive by its very nature—while the other vices are competitive only, so to speak, by accident. Pride gets no pleasure out of having something, only out of having more of it than the next man."

Do you find yourself playing the comparison game? Do you look at other people's abilities or possessions and feel resentment toward them? Not even Jesus could take pride in His abilities, but rather He said, "I can of mine own self do nothing." In Proverbs 18:12 we read, "Before his downfall a man's heart is proud, but humility comes before honor."

Don't let the Disease of Me spring up in your life!

—*Molly Ramseyer*

GAME PLAN

Ask God to search your heart and see if there is any offensive way in it. Confess to Him the people or things that you wish were yours.

From the Playbook:
Read Proverbs 16:5, 18; 18:12; 29:23.

EVEN IN LOSS

"May the name of the Lord be praised." Job 1:21

Becky Short was only a freshman when she qualified for the women's NCAA swim championships. When she mounted the starting blocks, her Auburn University team was in first place. It was the first time in history that Auburn women had led the meet, the first time every teammate had earned an All-American honor, and the first time an Auburn swimmer had broken an American record.

It was truly Auburn's shining moment. All Becky had to do was help her relay team finish in the Top 8 in prelims. A national title would be sure to follow. Under the pressure, though, Becky false started. Her relay team did not advance, and Auburn finished fourth overall.

Becky left the pool and hid, crushed that she had cost her team the championship. Her coach, David Marsh, found Becky and said she needed to return to the team. "That was the last place I wanted to be," Becky says. "How could they love me? I had let them down so terribly. But when I returned I found comfort, love, and encouragement."

Marsh took Becky aside. "He forgave me and reminded me that Jesus taught us to rejoice in our sufferings," Becky says. "Coach Marsh shared Job 2:10 with me, which says, 'Shall we accept good from God, and not trouble?' He added, 'The Lord gave and the Lord has taken away; may the name of the Lord be praised.'" (Job 1:20). This enabled her to work through the disappointment. The very next week she helped Auburn qualify for the world championships.

Even in loss, God is there. Look for Him.

— *Roxanne Robbins*

GAME PLAN

Think of a time you felt you failed. What did God teach you through that time?

From the Playbook:
Read Job 1–2.

STICKING OUT ALL OVER

"Let your shine before men, that they may see your good deeds and praise your Father." MATTHEW 5:16

When my niece, Alison, was four years old, she went with me to a nearby high school where I was scheduled to speak and demonstrate basketball skills to the students. On our way, I glanced over at her. She was dressed in a little warm-up suit, but I noticed that big tears were running down her cheeks. Quietly, she wiped them away.

I asked, "Alison, are you okay?"

She said, "My eyes are making me sad." I was surprised that she would have this feeling, because we would be only twenty minutes from her home.

To get her mind off this, I asked, "What do you think we should tell these people today?"

She said, "Let's tell them how to get Jesus in their hearts." In her four-year-old way, she told me that we needed to tell them to ask Jesus to forgive their sins, and then ask Him to come into their hearts. Wow! Proverbs 23:26 says, "My son, give me your heart and let your eyes keep to my ways."

A little later Alison asked me, "Aunt Tanya, how big is Jesus?"

To help her understand, I said, "Probably about as big as your dad."

With a puzzled look she said, "Aunt Tanya, when we ask Jesus into our hearts, isn't He going to stick out all over?" I laughed to myself.

Then I decided that she's right. I thought of Matthew 5:16, which says, "Let your light shine before men that they may see your good deeds and praise your Father in heaven." When Jesus is Lord of our lives, He permeates our thoughts, producing righteous actions and righteous words. In other words, He "sticks out all over."

—*Tanya Crevier, basketball showperson*

> **GAME PLAN**
>
> What are three specific ways you can influence others to consider the claim of Christ? Can you find three people for whom you can let your light shine?

From the Playbook:
Read Matthew 28:18–20.

WHO WANTS THE BLESSING?

"All these blessings will come upon you and accompany you if you obey the Lord your God." DEUTERONOMY 28:2

This was the hurdler's first and last junior high school state championship competition, and she wanted to win this race.

Her family, team, and coach were there to support her—confident in her ability. She was ready to run the best race of her life. She warmed up and answered the call to check in. Somehow, though, she missed the check-in. When the official called the names of the girls who would be racing, hers was not called.

Desperate, she ran to her coach for help. The meet director informed her coach that she had been told where to go, and she didn't show up. A miscommunication had taken place, and she was out of the race before it had even started. Devastation flooded the athlete, the team, her family, and her coach. All the hours of hard work were dashed because she did not respond correctly to the call, thereby putting her out of position for the race when called upon. The blessing of victory had escaped her.

How many times have God's blessings escaped us because we did not heed His call? Or we were not obedient to His will? How many missed opportunities have we passed because we did not respond correctly to His call? Blessings come when obedience to the voice of the Lord positions us to receive. We are all called to run the race of life, but we must obey the rules and not disqualify ourselves from the prize. Run your race to obtain the prize.

—*Madeline Mims, Olympic medalist, track*

GAME PLAN

"Father, help me to run the race of life by qualifying through Your Son, Jesus Christ. May I hear Your voice through Your Holy Word and obey You in all I do and say. Then, I will be positioned for the blessing of the prize and thereby bless others. Amen."

From the Playbook:
Read Deuteronomy 28 and 1 Corinthians 9:24–27.

MORE THAN YOU CAN HANDLE

"When I am weak, then I am strong." 2 CORINTHIANS 12:10

At age 21, LPGA pro Terry-Jo Myers was stricken with interstitial cystitis—a rare and painful bladder disease. For 11 years, she lived in constant and excruciating pain, keeping her condition a secret from everyone but her family.

When new medications relieved her pain, Terry-Jo planned a big "comeback," only to suffer two serious back injuries, both requiring surgery. After that, though, Terry-Jo was healthy again. She decided not to keep her struggles a secret. Whenever she has the opportunity, she tells her story in the hope of encouraging others who face difficulties of their own. Often, after hearing her speak, someone will exclaim, "I guess God never gives you more than you can handle!"

Terry-Jo understands what they mean. But she has to disagree. "It's *always* more than you can handle!" she says. "You're not ever supposed to get to where you don't need Him."

The truth is, there's no way we can handle the challenges of this life on our own, no matter how hard we try. God wants us to learn to depend on Him daily.

In 2 Corinthians 12:8, the apostle Paul talked about his struggle with a problem he called a "thorn" in his flesh: "Three times I pleaded with the Lord to take it away from me. But he said to me, 'My grace is sufficient for you, for my power is made perfect in weakness.'"

Is there something in your life that you can't handle? A problem you can't solve? Praise God for it! Because when we're weak, He is strong. God's grace really *is* sufficient. Let Him be your strength today.

—*Christin Ditchfield*

GAME PLAN

What is the biggest challenge you face today? Do you realize you can't handle it without God? Ask Him to help you with this situation. Pray for strength and grace.

From the Playbook:
Read 2 Corinthians 12:7–10 and Philippians 4:12–13.

SURPRISING BOLDNESS

"Enable your servants to speak your word with great boldness."
ACTS 4:29

On my first year of racing I got to stay at a race venue with another triathlete.

Sue had been at the top of the racing circuit for the previous few years. I was this shy rookie who couldn't believe her good fortune of staying with this legend.

One night Sue was flicking through the TV channels and stopped on *Touched by an Angel*. It was just at the point when the angel was lit up by God's light and was revealing herself to the woman she was assigned to help. Sue made some comment about this show being for "those crazy born-again Christians."

Well, somewhere out of this shy triathlete came the statement: "I'm a born-again Christian, and Jesus actually says in the Bible that 'no one can see the kingdom of God unless he is born again'" (John 3:3). I don't know who was more shocked at this boldness, her or me. I think it was me! When those words came out of my mouth, I sort of stepped out of myself and said, "Who is THAT girl!"

Up to this point I thought of my faith as a very personal thing. I was not bold in speaking God's truth, as I felt threatened by what others might think. To be bold with Sue was definitely out of my character. But that's the point. It was God's character and the guidance of the Holy Spirit enabling His servant to speak boldly.

The Lord can use the closeness that sports creates between competitors as a non-threatening way for each of us to speak His truth with great boldness.

—*Barb Lindquist, Olympic triathlete*

GAME PLAN

When in the past few days have you had a chance to be bold for Jesus and found your mouth glued shut? What can help to make sure the boldness Barb showed comes out next time?

From the Playbook:
Read 2 Corinthians 5:11–21.

GIVE IT ALL TO GOD

"Commit to the Lord whatever you do, and your plans will succeed." PROVERBS 16:3

On April 1994, I traveled to Boston, Massachusetts, for the Boston Marathon. I had won this prestigious event the previous 4 years, and I was more excited than ever to be returning to this race.

Three days before the marathon, I went out to eat with several people at a local restaurant. The next morning, I woke up feeling dizzy and nauseated. A phone call from a friend informed me that seven other people in our party of fourteen were dealing with the effects of food poisoning too.

The day before the marathon, I was still feeling bad, and I was beginning to despair as I thought about the next day's event. As I read my Bible, I came across Proverbs 16:3, which says, "Commit to the Lord whatever you do, and your plans will succeed." I knew this was not a guarantee of success, but right then and there I committed my race to God. I would leave the "success" part up to Him.

GAME PLAN

Why should you commit everything to God? What are the guarantees? What does it suggest about your relationship with Him?

Amazingly, though I felt like pulling out of the race on several occasions, I won my fifth straight Boston Marathon and broke the world record in the women's wheelchair division with a time of 1 hour, 34 minutes, 22 seconds. That record still stood through the 2007 race.

Since that event, I have committed everything to God: every workout, race, interview, speaking engagement, and whatever else. When I give every situation to God, the pressure is off me, regardless of the outcome.

—*Jean Driscoll, eight-time Boston Marathon wheelchair champion*

From the Playbook:
Read 1 Corinthians 1:4–9.

FOCUS ABOVE

"Do not worry about tomorrow, for tomorrow will worry about itself." MATTHEW 6:34

It was the beginning of April 2004, and the WNBA draft was coming up in a couple of weeks. So many thoughts were running through my head. Would I be drafted? What team would I go to? Am I good enough to make the team? Will I like my teammates and coaches? How would I adjust to a new environment?

It was a very stressful time and a scary situation. My college career at Boston College had gone well, but now it was time to look at the future. In a few weeks I could possibly be going to the WNBA, or I could be trying to find a job in the real world. It was all so exciting yet so nerve-racking at the same time. What was going to happen?

As I look back on it now, I know I worried way too much throughout these weeks. After being drafted in the third round by the Minnesota Lynx and then making the team, I asked myself why I had worried and made myself become so stressed and anxious. After all, the Lord knew His will for my life and what the outcome would be.

This was a good lesson for me to remember. It reminded me to keep my eyes on the Lord and to only worry about today. God is in total control, and He will provide; all we have to do is seek Him, and He will take care of the rest.

So, when you are feeling overwhelmed about situations in the future, remember to seek God and obey His ways. Do not let your worries about tomorrow affect your relationship with the Lord today!

—*Amber Jacobs, former WBNA guard*

GAME PLAN

What are you worrying about today? Does worrying change anything? If this situation entails action, take it. If it entails waiting, then turn it over to God and let Him handle it. If He needs your help, He'll let you know. Note how many times the word "worry" appears in the Playbook passage.

From the Playbook:
Read Matthew 6:25–34.

&%*$#@*!!

"The mouth of the fool gushes folly." PROVERBS 15:2

"I've been waitin' forty-five minutes for a blankety-blank pizza. That's too blankety-blank long." That was the flame-broiled reply from a fellow pizza store patron after I calmly said, "Sure taking a long time for the pizza, isn't it?"

Later that evening, I was watching a baseball game on TV. The umpires, those normally stellar icons of accuracy and perfection, blew a couple of calls. Missed 'em by a mile. Next thing I knew, I could hear tens of thousands of fans yelling in the background, "&%*$#@*&!"

That same week, I overheard some Christian kids talking about something they didn't like. "That *blanks,*" they complained, using a term that was not long ago considered filthy enough to get kids kicked out of school for uttering.

So what's the big deal? Does it really matter, anyway? Don't we have more important things to consider than a few naughty words? Well, if we take the Bible seriously, no.

How can we ignore verses like these: "It is shameful even to mention what the disobedient do in secret" (Ephesians 5:12). "Nor should there be obscenity, foolish talk or coarse joking, which are out of place" (5:4). "You shall not misuse the name of the Lord your God" (Exodus 20:7). "You must rid yourselves of . . . filthy language" (Colossians 3:8).

We can't always avoid hearing bad language—especially in sports. But if we understand that "filthy language" dishonors God, we'll begin to see how important it is that we keep our own words clean. We'll avoid letting ourselves become so conditioned that bad words don't bother us anymore.

—Dave Branon

GAME PLAN

What are some words you find yourself using that you know are not honoring to the Lord? How can your relationship with God help you keep your language clean? Do you think you can watch movies and TV with bad language and not have it affect you? Can you justify that stance biblically?

From the Playbook:
Read James 3:1–12.

SHINE LIKE A BIG OLD STAR

"Humble yourselves, therefore, under God's mighty hand."
1 PETER 5:6

Do you long to be the star on your team? As highly driven athletes, sometimes we push too hard to attain perfection and be the star. We lose our perspective on the kingdom of God.

I remember hearing a testimony from a minor league baseball player, and it really challenged me. I was asking if he was getting much playing time. His answer to me was, "No, God has me in the bullpen."

I was a little confused. Why would God want him on the bench? Is that success? My perspective was way off! I was amazed at how content this player was to be on the bench. He was content because he was more concerned with God's plan than his own. He was God's light in the bullpen.

God has a purpose for every situation. We need to humble ourselves daily, seek after God, and keep His perspective. He will give us peace and give us opportunities to shine for His glory, not our own.

I love the second part of 1 Peter 5:6! It says, "he may lift you up in due time." This lifting up may not be from a physical standpoint, but then again it might.

I believe that God allowed me to be the first woman to hit an out-of-the-park home run in the history of baseball. It was to be used for His glory, and it was a way for my Father to bless His child. It has given me great opportunity to shine bright for Him.

May we all long to be the brightest star in the kingdom of God. Matthew 5:16 tells us, "Let your light shine before men, that they may see your good deeds and praise your Father in heaven." We never shine brighter than when we are reflecting God's glory.

—*Kim Braatz-Voisard, former pro baseball player*

GAME PLAN

Name three specific ways you can shine bright for God—showing others the light of God's presence. Then plan to make those three things happen.

From the Playbook:
Read Matthew 5:13–16.

ONLY ON SUNDAY?

"Live as children of light." EPHESIANS 5:8

One controversy in professional sports today is the matter of prayer on the field. Sometimes after a big play or a victory, a player will drop to his knees and thank God. Some people object to this practice.

One newspaper writer suggested that the playing fields should be off-limits to such religious practices. He said that anything having to do with God should be confined to church. To him, it's "absolutely ridiculous" for people to talk to God anywhere else.

As Christians, we would disagree with this kind of thinking. But we sometimes give the impression by our behavior that we believe it. We set Sundays aside to worship and serve God, but then we act as if the rest of the week is ours to do with as we please.

Now here's the point that nonbelievers fail to understand: For the believer in Jesus Christ, living for God is a 24-hours-a-day, 7-days-a-week proposition. Notice Paul's teaching in Ephesians 5. When he talked about walking "as children of light" (v. 8), he wasn't referring only to the way we behave in church on Sundays. When we are filled with the Spirit, we will exemplify compassion, kindness, humility, forgiveness, thankfulness, and love. Not just for an hour or two on Sunday, but all the time.

The Christian life is not for Sunday only. It's a day-to-day, all-the-time way of life—even on the playing field.

— *Dave Branon*

GAME PLAN

Think about what part of the week finds you acting least like a Christian. Dedicate that time period to God, and ask Him to make you godly even then.

From the Playbook:
Read Ephesians 5:8–21.

WHOSE POWER IS IT?

" 'Not by might nor by power, but by my Spirit,' says the Lord."
ZECHARIAH 4:6

On a previous devotional (page 50) I mentioned *Touched by an Angel*, the TV program. Today, we'll talk about Touched by an Angel—the real thing. We read in Zechariah 4:6 that an angel of God gave a word for Zerubbabel through the prophet Zechariah.

Zerubbabel was in charge of rebuilding the temple of Jerusalem after the Jews returned from captivity in Babylon. The angel was speaking words of encouragement to Zerubbabel, as the rebuilding process had been slow at best. Through the angelic visitor, God reminded Z that the people's might and power wouldn't be able to do the job alone. The Lord said it was only through working in His Spirit that the temple at Jerusalem would be rebuilt.

As athletes we are led to believe that the toughest, strongest, and even meanest will survive and win. Yes, sometimes we can win a race on just our own brute strength and sheer muscular power, but winning is not the sole purpose of racing. Only things done in the Spirit have any lasting, eternal significance.

Shouldn't that be the goal in all we do? We won't grow in our relationship with God by relying on our own might and power. God can lead us, encourage us, and mold us into the champions—both in and out of competition—that He wants us to be. It is from doing this that we become champions for God.

— *Barb Lindquist, Olympic triathlete*

GAME PLAN

Feeling inadequate? Join the club. Then turn it over to God to give you the strength and power you need.

From the Playbook:
Read Zechariah 4.

HOLY COW!

"Be holy, because I am holy." 1 Peter 1:16

Legendary baseball announcer Harry Caray made the phrase "Holy Cow" famous. "Holy Cow! He struck him out!" he would say. We also hear people talk about "Holy Toledo!" (If you live there, you know it's not true.)

But when it comes to true holiness—well, it's a far cry from animals or cities. The concept of being holy is something we need to examine with seriousness and concern. How can we not? Scripture clearly quotes God as saying, "Be holy, because I am holy."

We also read these pronouncements about holiness in the Bible: "You ought to live holy and godly lives" (2 Peter 3:11). "Make every effort to live in peace with all men and to be holy" (Hebrews 12:14). "God . . . has saved us and called us to a holy life" (2 Timothy 1:8-9).

Sounds monklike, doesn't it? There is no doubt, though, that God has put holy living out there as a goal we are to reach for.

So, what does it mean? Here's what an 18th-century Christian writer named William Law said about it: "This, and this alone, is Christianity, a universal holiness in every part of life, a heavenly wisdom in all our actions, not conforming in the spirit and temper of the world but turning all worldly enjoyments into means of piety and devotion to God."

In a society that doesn't think much of Christian piety and devotion to God and His Word, this is a double challenge. But it is possible.

Cows aren't holy and neither is Toledo. But you can be.

—Dave Branon

GAME PLAN

Do you equate holy with "no fun" and "boring"? How can you think differently? Do you know anyone whose life seems to be marked by the kind of holiness you'd like to experience?

From the Playbook:
Read Hebrews 10:1-10.

GOD HAS PLANS FOR YOU

"I have . . . plans to prosper you and not to harm you."
JEREMIAH 29:11

GAME PLAN

Write in your journal about something that didn't go the way you wanted it to. How did God turn the situation into good?

During her 18-year professional tennis career, Zina Garrison won 14 titles and became one of 12 women to win 500 matches. At age 26 she reached a No. 4 world ranking and became the first African-American tennis player since Althea Gibson in 1958 to reach a Grand Slam final. Also one of the finest doubles players in recent history, Zina and her playing partner, Pam Shriver, won gold in the 1988 Seoul Olympics.

After Zina retired from pro tennis, her life took a dramatic turn. "I went through a series of struggles for a couple of years," Zina says. "Now, however, I can see that despite the pain, it was really an awesome pilgrimage. My faith in God grew even stronger because in the midst of all the trials and tribulations I faced, He was there. I grew to understand that God would always pull me through. Even if no one else is there for me, Jesus always is. When I thought I couldn't get through or didn't have anyone there, I would pray and later on see how things materialized. Everything didn't always turn out the way I wanted it to, but in God's timing things always did work out."

Garrison has come to a new place spiritually. The 2000 US Olympic tennis coach has accepted that life does not always go the way she plans it, but she now has confidence that God is in control. As she looks ahead, she can more patiently wait on His leading and then make the most of the opportunities God brings her way.

Like Zina, we must put our trust in God in front of any plans we have—for we know He wants what is best for us.

— *Roxanne Robbins*

From the Playbook:
Read Jeremiah 29:11–14.

GIVING GOD THE HONOR

"Those who honor me I will honor." 1 SAMUEL 2:30

Have you ever picked up a *Sports Illustrated* and been pleasantly surprised to find a story about an athlete who embraces the Christian faith? Have you been refreshed when you turned on the television and observed a person testifying about the role Jesus Christ plays in his or her life? Why did this affect you?

First, it probably surprised you to observe someone's faith articulated through the mainstream media. And it put a smile on your face because you knew thousands of people could be seeing a glimpse of our Savior. Many Christian athletes talk openly to the media about their relationship with Christ. Other Christian athletes, even when given the right opportunity, will choose not to acknowledge God publicly. They may refrain because they are young believers and not yet strong enough to handle the public expectations that accompany statements of faith. Or reporters may not ask them a question that gives them room to mention faith.

There are many legitimate reasons Christian athletes may not mention their faith each time a microphone is placed in front of them. Realizing this, 2000 USA Olympic heptathlete Dee Dee Nathan says she knows there are times when she must rely on actions and not words. Her goal, however, is never to be embarrassed about talking about her Savior. "I pray for boldness and confidence to proclaim the gospel," Nathan says. "I lean on the second part of 1 Samuel 2:30, which says, 'Those who honor me I will honor, but those who despise me will be disdained.'"

How will you choose to honor God today?

—*Roxanne Robbins*

GAME PLAN

When was the last time you had a chance to articulate your faith in Christ but held back because of embarrassment? Talk to the Lord about the situation and ask Him to give you wisdom and boldness to know when and what to say in the future.

From the Playbook:
Read Psalm 15.

GOD HAS NO GRANDCHILDREN

"Choose for yourselves . . . whom you will serve." JOSHUA 24:15

Growing up, WNBA superstar Ruthie Bolton spent a lot of time shooting hoops. Basketball was one of the few games she and her nineteen siblings could all play together! When Ruthie proved to be a gifted athlete, she was following a family tradition (several of her brothers and sisters were successful college athletes). In a sense, the same was true of her Christian faith. Ruthie's father was a pastor; so are five of her brothers.

But no one gets into heaven because of his or her family's faith. A relationship with Jesus Christ isn't something you can inherit. As Joshua explained to the children of Israel, serving God is a personal decision. It's something you have to choose for yourself.

Ruthie discovered this truth soon after she graduated from high school. "When I was seven, I had asked Jesus to be my Savior," she says. "But later on, I wondered if I was just living right because I had to. It wasn't really optional at our house," she explains. "I wondered how it would be when times got tough, or when I was out on my own. In college, I found myself facing all kinds of obstacles, all kinds of challenges. When I reached back to draw on the faith and values that my father had instilled in me, then I realized that God really had saved me and that He really was with me!"

What about you? Can you truly call your faith your own?

—*Christin Ditchfield*

GAME PLAN

Can you recall a specific time when you made the choice to receive Jesus Christ as your personal Savior and live for Him? If not, do it today!

From the Playbook:
Read Joshua 24:14–18.

EAGLES ON THE RISE

"Those who hope in the Lord will renew their strength."
ISAIAH 40:31

In basketball, point guard is the toughest position on the court. Not only do you have to call the play, tell players what to do and where to go, and keep the tempo, but you also have to handle the ball while a defender is pressuring you. Many teams are successful because they have a great point guard who runs the show.

A good point guard allows everyone else to feel relaxed and comfortable, takes the pressure off others, and steps into a leadership role. I love being a point guard and having that control and command. However, there are times throughout my basketball career when I feel as if I cannot handle the role of being a point guard. I feel a weight on my shoulders and a built-up pressure that causes stress and anxiety.

Where will I find the energy, the stamina, and the mental toughness needed to lead my team at the point guard position when that happens? I know I cannot afford to be exhausted and overwhelmed, but I am. However, God is never too tired nor too busy to help, listen, and be my source of strength.

When you are feeling engulfed by stress or feeling uneasy because of a tough assignment ahead—stop, breathe, and pray. Although you are weary, God's power and strength never fade. As I have learned time and time again, we need to look to the Lord to renew our strength. He knows that we are overwhelmed with pressures and stress throughout the day or through the circumstances He puts us through. Yet we have a hope and joy in the Lord that allows us to call upon Him—regaining strength and soaring "like eagles" in His love (Isaiah 40:31).

—*Amber Jacobs, former WNBA guard*

GAME PLAN

What's your stress factor? Is it as Amber describes in her job as a point guard—sometimes overwhelming? Have you thought about turning it over to God?

From the Playbook:
Read Isaiah 40:27–31.

NEVER ALONE

"Where can I go from your Spirit? Where can I flee from your presence?" PSALM 139:7

I'm standing on the baseline alongside the rest of my Cleveland Rockers teammates in New York's Madison Square Garden as the National Anthem is being sung. As I stand there with my hand across my heart, I am reminded of the importance of the song and its comforting sound.

Several years before, I was standing next to different teammates listening to an unfamiliar anthem. That was in Launceston, Tasmania, the little island off the bottom of Australia. I headed "Down Under" to play professionally the winter following my senior year in college. It was there that I truly realized the necessity of my relationship with Jesus Christ.

Although I accepted Christ when I was eleven, I never gave complete control over to Him. I always had my family to lean on in times of need.

That comfort zone suddenly changed when I boarded a 14-hour flight to Australia. Now placed in a situation completely on my own, I learned what it meant to be alone. I chose to turn to the Lord and open my Bible. I began to study the meaning behind the verses. I found a nice Baptist church that took me in as one of their own. But most important, I continued to pray. God was there. I could feel His presence, His comfort, compassion, and love. The Lord's Spirit overfilled my heart.

I made the effort to seek Him. That's all it took. I realized He was always there. I just hadn't been paying much attention.

Jesus Christ is in my life and heart everywhere I go. Whether I was in Orlando, Florida, or Tasmania, I knew I was not alone.

—*Tricia Binford, former WNBA guard*

GAME PLAN

Are there some places you go where you feel Jesus is not with you or is not as close? What can you do to make sure that doesn't happen?

From the Playbook:
Read Psalm 139.

REAL HOPE

"We wait for the blessed hope—the glorious appearing of our great God and Savior, Jesus Christ." Titus 2:13

It has been said that as oxygen is to the lungs, so hope is to the human heart. We need hope. What is real hope? Perhaps you can recall an occasion in your past when you failed to study for an exam. When someone asked you whether or not you passed, you responded, "I hope so." That type of hope could better be described as baseless optimism. Because you did not properly prepare for the exam, you have no reasonable grounds for confidence that your desires will be fulfilled. You are simply exercising wishful thinking.

Biblical hope is trustful expectation. It is the confidence that God will do what He said He would do. Titus 2:13–14 reads, "while we wait for the blessed hope—the glorious appearing of our great God and Savior, Jesus Christ, who gave himself for us to redeem us from all wickedness."

What do you draw hope from? What is it that keeps you going and gives you reason to live? Many people rely on false hope or simply on wishful thinking. They may depend upon wealth, possessions, accomplishment, good deeds, or their righteousness. While these may temporarily energize us, there is no sustaining ability for the long term, much less for eternity.

GAME PLAN

List three things that give you hope. Sometimes we need things that give us something to look forward to. How can you make sure your key hope is in God?

Peter writes in 1 Peter 1:3, "In his great mercy he has given us new birth into a living hope through the resurrection of Jesus Christ from the dead." Real hope can only be found through our faith and trust in the death, burial, and resurrection of Jesus Christ. If we are placing our hope in anything else, it is simply wishful thinking.

—*Bill Sampen, former major league pitcher*

From the Playbook:
Read Titus 2.

THE HUGGERS

"Greet one another with a holy kiss." ROMANS **16:16**

All right. Now that I've got your attention with all this mushy stuff about hugging and kissing, let's get down to business. I have an important point to make.

Nearly 3,000 athletes take part in the summer games of Michigan's Special Olympics. The slogan of the Special Olympics is this: "Caring is more important than winning." This is especially true of those competitors who are mentally impaired.

The events at the Special Olympics are like any other track meet—with one major difference. At the finish line is a group of volunteers the Olympic Committee calls "huggers." Their job, in addition to calling out the winners, is to encourage one of the competitors throughout the race and to greet him or her at the finish line with a big hug. The real secret to the success of the games is love.

These huggers remind me of what's going on in Romans 16. There Paul gave special recognition to the men and women who had been "running the race" for the Lord so diligently in Rome. He didn't flatter them or heap praise on them. He didn't give them a trophy for "Best Church Worker in the World." But he did remember them by name. He gave them confidence by approving their work.

Paul would have made a good "hugger." (Actually, the text mentioned kissing, but you know how cultures change.)

Perhaps you can be that kind of encourager too. Let a friend know how much you appreciate it when he or she compliments you. Express appreciation to a co-worker who's been especially kind. Somehow, let the love of Jesus show through. Make those around you feel like winners.

—*Mart DeHaan*

GAME PLAN

Get out the old stationery and write a note to someone who needs a written hug from you.

From the Playbook:
Read Romans 16:1–16.

LET GOD WORK ON YOU

"Yet, O Lord, you are our Father. We are the clay, you are the potter; we are all the work of your hand." Isaiah 64:8

So many people put a delay on giving their lives to Christ because they feel they have to get right first. The reality is this: We cannot get ourselves right before God. We must humble ourselves and come to Him, knowing that He is the author of perfection. The change that we desire can be accomplished only through Jesus Christ.

Then there are some people who refuse to believe because they think the person they were yesterday is the person they have to be today. This limiting belief will keep them imprisoned to their past mistakes and limitations. When we come to Christ as we are, we relinquish our power and allow Him to reconstruct our lives.

One great example of that in Scripture is the concept that God is the potter and we are the clay. The more we yield to Him, the more He is able to shape and mold us into what He wants us to be.

Another illustration of our need to be connected to God is in John 15, where Jesus says, "I am the true vine, and my Father is the gardener. He cuts off every branch in me that bears no fruit . . . Remain in me, and I will remain in you. No branch can bear fruit by itself; it must remain in the vine" (vv. 1–4).

All we have to do is come to Him as we are. The transformation of our old selves into spiritual beings is a process. If we allow God to do the transforming in our lives, we can rest assured that we will be all that God created us to be.

—*Charlotte Smith, former WNBA forward*

GAME PLAN

Have you surrendered your life to Christ completely to let Him mold you and help you bear fruit? If not, you need to do that.

From the Playbook:

Read more about the vine and the branches in John 15:1–14.

ACHE I: HOW'S YOUR *ATTITUDE*?

"Your attitude should be the same as that of Christ Jesus: Who being in very nature God, did not consider equality with God something to be grasped." PHILIPPIANS 2:5

All athletes share one element of sports: pain. Whether it is the soreness of a weekend warrior who did too much, a Little Leaguer whose team lost the championship game, or a pro athlete who pushed himself too hard—they all feel the aches and pains of athletic competition.

The Christian life is compared to an athletic event in the New Testament (Acts 20:24; Romans 9:3; 1 Corinthians 9:24; Galatians 2:2; 5:7; 2 Timothy 4:7; Hebrews 12:1), an event that sometimes can seem painful. Over the next four days we will examine four attributes of Christian maturity that will help keep our perspective when trouble hits. These attributes can be remembered through the acronym "ACHE."

Attitude is the first attribute we will examine. The dictionary defines attitude as "one's disposition, opinion or mental set." In Philippians 2:5–8, Paul encourages us to have the Christlike mindset of humility. In this way, Paul reminds us that we can be our own biggest enemy. When we focus on our own needs, it is easy for us to have a selfish attitude. If this is our way of thinking, we miss the point of the Christian message.

Jesus Christ is to be our example as we grow in maturity. He never considered His own needs, but He obeyed the Father in doing His duty of going to the cross on behalf of humankind. As a result, God will exalt Him so that everyone will honor Jesus in the resurrection.

This example is given to us so that we also will demonstrate humility and consider others better than ourselves. That's the right attitude.

—*Kyle Abbott, former major league pitcher*

GAME PLAN

When do you struggle with your attitude? Isn't it most often when something happens that doesn't go your way? That's an attitude of immaturity.

From the Playbook:
Read Philippians 2:1–11.

ACHE 2: ARE YOU *CONCENTRATING*?

"I press on toward the goal to win the prize for which God has called me." PHILIPPIANS 3:14

The second letter in ACHE that reminds us of how to keep our perspective during difficult times is C—for **Concentration**.

When trials arise, how do you handle them? In Philippians, Paul writes to churchgoers who were suffering persecution for their faith. In fact, Paul himself wrote from a prison cell. His advice to his readers (and to us) is to face trials joyfully. This is not something we do automatically. It takes patience and practice. Our responsibility is to remain focused and to keep the prize of heaven before us.

In Philippians 3:12–14, Paul instructs us to "press on." In verses 13 and 14 he writes, "I do not consider myself yet to have taken hold of it. But one thing I do: Forgetting what is behind and straining toward what is ahead, I press on toward the goal to win the prize for which God has called me heavenward in Christ Jesus." Paul continued to maintain a single-minded focus on his future. The New Living Translation renders it this way, "I am focusing all my energies on this one thing: Forgetting the past and looking forward to what lies ahead, I strain to reach the end of the race and receive the prize": eternal life with Christ.

GAME PLAN

What do you spend most of your time concentrating on? Is God even in the Top Five? What are a couple of ways you can increase your concentration on God?

In sports, we use the term "in the zone" to describe the ultimate in concentration. Paul desired to be in the zone in regard to his Christian life.

Has anything replaced the zeal you once had for Christ? Take Paul's advice and lay it aside and pursue "the goal."

— *Kyle Abbott, former major league pitcher*

From the Playbook:
Read Psalm 42.

ACHE 3: DO YOU HAVE *HOPE?*

"Our citizenship is in heaven." PHILIPPIANS 3:20

Paul gives us some practical advice for handling trials. As we continue to look at the acronym ACHE, we can see that in order to have the right **Attitude** and maintain **Concentration**, we move to the letter H—**Hope**. The message of Christianity is one of hope. Because Jesus rose from the dead, we can be assured that God can do anything in our lives.

In Philippians 3:18–21, Paul compares unbelievers and believers and tells believers that they are citizens of heaven. We should live with hope that no matter what happens in our lives God will transform us into the glorious body in which we will live forever.

If our hope is based on anything other than Jesus Christ, then that hope is vain. This is because the power that raised Christ from the dead is the same power that is available to us. God's desire is for us to have proper perspective when we face trials.

In comparison to eternity with Him, anything we face in life is minor. Paul said, "I consider everything a loss compared to the surpassing greatness of knowing Christ Jesus my Lord, for whose sake I have lost all things. I consider them rubbish, that I may gain Christ and be found in him, not having a righteousness of my own that comes from the law, but that which is through faith in Christ—the righteousness that comes from God and is by faith. I want to know Christ and the power of his resurrection and the fellowship of sharing in his sufferings, becoming like him in his death, and so, somehow, to attain to the resurrection from the dead" (Philippians 3:8–11).

—*Kyle Abbott, former major league pitcher*

GAME PLAN

What do you think hope means in a spiritual context? Do you have the absolute sure hope of eternal life? With faith in Christ, you can.

From the Playbook:
Read Hebrews 6:13–20.

ACHE 4: ARE YOU MAKING AN *EFFORT*?

"Continue to work out your salvation." PHILIPPIANS 2:12

The final letter in the acronym ACHE is E for **Effort**.

In Philippians 2:12–16, Paul reminds us that we must "continue to work out our salvation with fear and trembling." The greatest part of this message is that God "works in us to will and to act according to his good purpose" (Philippians 2:13). This tells us that when the circumstances of our life make it the most difficult to follow God, He is the one sustaining us. This is the effort that we are to give. Our responsibility is to maintain fellowship with Him, so that we can be vessels of His grace to others.

A second aspect of this verse that is related to our witness for Christ is that we are to "Do everything without complaining or arguing" (v. 14). The image Paul presents when we make this kind of effort is that we shine like stars. People watch the way we behave. People do not care what we say if our actions do not bear the same witness. With this in mind, the effort that we make to keep the proper attitude, concentrating on the goal, with the hope of our heavenly citizenship before us, allows us to demonstrate Christlikeness to an unbelieving world.

This is why Paul was able to remain joyful in spite of troubling circumstances. He withstood the aches of life with the ACHE of Jesus Christ. It was his mindset, his goal, his hope, and his endeavor. This is how we also can achieve victory no matter what circumstances we face.

— *Kyle Abbott, former major league pitcher*

GAME PLAN

Have you come to grips with the fact that you cannot do anything to earn your salvation, yet God expects us to not be lazy in our faith? What are you doing as a witness of your faith to others?

From the Playbook:
Read James 2:14–26.

69

TARA'S TIPS

"I seek you with all my heart." PSALM 119:10

When tennis teen Tara Snyder joined the WTA Tour, she expected to become a big star. Instead, Snyder suffered some tough losses, made some embarrassing mistakes, and felt like giving up. But she persevered. Four years later, she earned her first title and cracked the Top 50 in the rankings.

Even with all its challenges, life on the Tour has been a great experience for Tara. Here's what she says she learned:

1. Stay focused. "Sports are so competitive! To reach the top you really have to be motivated, even driven, to give it your best every day."

2. Surround yourself with positive, spiritual people. "My boyfriend, my coach, and my agent are all Christians. They don't put a lot of pressure on me to win or make money. They want to see me grow spiritually. They encourage me and pray for me, and their support keeps me headed in the right direction."

3. Ask God. "When I'm struggling with something personally or trying to make tough decisions about my schedule or my career, I pray. Waking up in the morning and going to bed at night—even sitting on a plane, I ask God to show me what He wants me to do. He knows what's best."

4. Most important, put Him first. "Before tennis, before anything else in my life, my faith in God comes first. I know that when I put my trust in Him, everything else will take care of itself."

Tara has learned some valuable lessons we all can apply to our lives!

—*Christin Ditchfield*

GAME PLAN

Look over Tara's tips and see which ones you can apply to your life today. Or make your own list of three or four life lessons you've learned lately.

From the Playbook:

Read Psalm 119:9–16, 33–37.

MENTORS AND FRIENDS

*"Now you are the body of Christ, and each one of you
is a part of it."* 1 Corinthians 12:27

When I first arrived on the scene in the LPGA, I was fortunate to be able to get to know mature Christian golfers such as Betsy King and Barb Mucha. They were just what I needed, because they helped me understand the golf scene as a Christian—with the right perspective.

Barb was an especially key Christian friend my first few years on Tour. Now I can return the favor to others. I feel compelled to mentor the rookies coming out on the Tour and give them a sense of security and support as their sister in Christ.

I have invited numerous rookies to our Bible Fellowship for a chance to meet some of the players in a noncompetitive setting. A few years ago I invited Jamie Hullett to join me for Fellowship. Jamie can come across as very shy and quiet. She seemed to enjoy the message and the fellowship, but because of how quiet she was I didn't know she was already a Christian. She is a very strong follower of Christ and just goes about her walk in a quiet manner.

One year I invited Jody Niemann-Dansie to the group. Jody was not a Christian but through some mentoring by Siew-Ai Lim, Jody and her husband, Bryan, became Christians that summer. I simply bridged the gap and befriended Jody by going to dinner and playing practice rounds with her. Then Siew-Ai, who has much more mentoring knowledge than I do, had one-on-one Bible study times with Jody.

That's how the body is supposed to work—all working toward a common cause: to let others know the great love Christ has to offer us.

—*Wendy Ward, LPGA golfer*

> **GAME PLAN**
>
> List three people you might be able to mentor over time. What steps can you take to begin to help them grow spiritually?

From the Playbook:
Read 2 Timothy 2:1–15.

DON'T LET IT GO TO YOUR HEAD

"Consider everything [else] a loss." PHILIPPIANS 3:8

Since making the USA Women's Basketball National Team and starring in the WNBA, Ruthie Bolton has lived a life that women athletes used to only dream about. She and her teammates have traveled the world, received lucrative endorsements, jogged with the President, and won two Olympic gold medals.

If you were in Ruthie's, or another star athletes' shoes, how would you keep the success, money, and awards in perspective? Wouldn't it be easy to let it all go to your head?

To stay grounded, Ruthie clings to the truth of Philippians 3:8, which says, "I consider everything a loss compared to the surpassing greatness of knowing Christ Jesus my Lord, for whose sake I have lost all things."

"My spiritual background and being a Christian has really helped me as far as keeping a great attitude and realizing I can't take this too seriously," Ruthie says. "I need to take basketball seriously to a certain point, but also realize this is all background music. The most important thing is to do right and please God."

By "background music," Ruthie means basketball is something that has added happiness to her life but does not make up the core of who she is. She uses a musical analogy to describe her perspective on sports because she is also a gifted singer. Performing gospel songs at various venues is a way for Ruthie to give thanks for a Christian faith that has enabled her to deal with life's pressures.

What talents has God given you? How can you use those talents for His glory?

—*Roxanne Robbins*

GAME PLAN

Is there something in your life that is overshadowing your walk with the Lord? If so, ask God to help you prioritize your thoughts and time so that you can fully experience the surpassing greatness of knowing Christ.

From the Playbook:
Read Philippians 3:1–11.

GET TOGETHER WITH GOD

*"My heart says of you, 'Seek his face!' Your face, Lord,
I will seek."* PSALM 27:8

You make it look so easy and graceful."

I have heard this comment about my golf swing many times. Often my response is this: "I have played golf for many years, hitting thousands of golf balls, stroking thousands of putts, and competing in several hundred tournaments."

I say that because I have practiced and spent mountains of time developing a graceful swing. It just didn't happen the first time I played golf. I have chosen to spend time honing my golf skills and in return I have been blessed with the opportunity to play professionally. When I don't spend time practicing, I find it difficult to stay consistent on the course. So I must spend time practicing daily to stay competitive.

I believe the same principle applies to our relationship with God. A strong relationship with Him does not just spring up overnight. One of the reasons God wants us to spend quality time with Him is so that we can get to know Him better.

We can do that by studying and reading the Bible, and by learning from mature Christians. Just as I must listen carefully to my golf coach in order to improve my game, we must also spend time talking to and listening to God. Through intimate moments with Him we grow, we change, we're encouraged, and we find rest. The psalm writer David said, "My heart says of you, 'Seek his face!' Your face, Lord, I will seek" (27:8).

Seek His face daily and allow your spirit to be refreshed and renewed.

—*Tracy Hanson, former LPGA golfer*

GAME PLAN

Have you spent time with God today? Get out your schedule right now and set aside 30 minutes for each of the next 5 days to enjoy God's company. Read Scripture, pray, or just listen to God.

From the Playbook:
Read Psalm 34:1–10 to discover some of the benefits
of spending time with God.

MIXED SIGNALS

"Do not be yoked together with unbelievers."
2 CORINTHIANS 6:14

You would think the American Cancer Society would be more careful. But someone wasn't paying attention to details when the ACS decided to hold a benefit night in conjunction with a professional tennis tournament.

That sounds pretty safe, tennis being excellent exercise for a healthy heart and all. Things started to turn embarrassing, though, when the ACS discovered that a major tobacco company was sponsoring the competition. Although they weren't aware of it, officials of the society had committed themselves to selling 500 tickets to an event that was named after a well-known brand of cigarettes. By the time they found out, it was too late.

So, here was a group that was asking people to quit smoking, yet sending out publicity that portrayed a young woman with a tennis racket in one hand and a cigarette in the other. It was a classic example of mixed signals.

Just as cigarettes and the American Cancer Society don't mix, neither do Christians and some of our entanglements. For example, if you start dating a person who has no interest in God or biblical morality, you are sending mixed signals.

Paul stated in 2 Corinthians 6:14 that God's children must restrict their close fellowship to those who see things as they do. Why? Because righteousness and wickedness have nothing in common. Whenever there are mixed signals, the message is garbled.

Remember, God's Word says that Christ and His enemy have nothing in common. So, let's be careful not to be "yoked together" with those who favor Satan's agenda over the Lord's.

—*Mart DeHaan*

GAME PLAN

List your five closest relationships. If any of those people are not fellow believers, how can you try to win them over without compromising your standards?

From the Playbook:
Read 2 Corinthians 6:14–16.

YOU NEED TEAMMATES

"Though all its parts are many, they form one body."
1 CORINTHIANS 12:12

We as Christians are called to be good "teammates." This applies not only in the arena of athletics but also in our day-to-day lives. What makes a good teammate in God's eyes?

- A good teammate sees the big picture, which is not about self-satisfaction and individual honors, but rather the goal of the group.
- A good teammate is someone who puts the team's goals ahead of his or her own and is unselfish in serving others with respect.
- A good teammate has complete faith in the leader and is obedient.
- A good teammate does everything with diligence, passion, joy, and appreciation.
- A good teammate knows his or her role and performs his or her best, without envy or pride.

GAME PLAN

What kind of a teammate are you? Do people see you as self-centered or others-centered? When you talk, do you mostly talk about you, or do you allow others to feel important? What can you do to be a better companion, teammate, sister, daughter, wife, friend?

We all have different roles and different talents that God specifically gave us to use for His purposes on His team! We must know our roles and use our talents for His purposes, knowing that however big or small that role, we all are an important part of the body of Christ.

We all need each other, and we all are needed for the proper functioning of His kingdom.

—*Jenny Boucek, coach, WNBA*

From the Playbook:
Read 1 Corinthians 12:12–27.

GOD IS IN CONTROL

"Do not be anxious about anything." PHILIPPIANS 4:6

It was getting down to crunch time. I was on the USA national volleyball team, and we were only one month away from our Olympic qualifying tournament.

I realized my priorities were a bit mixed up when I received a call from my doctor just minutes before I was to leave for practice. She told me that a mole removed from my chest had come back positive for malignant melanoma. My first reaction was, "Can we take care of this in about a month?" She replied, "This could be life-threatening." I was shocked by her words.

After she explained the seriousness of melanoma, I understood that this was something I needed to take care of immediately. I realized I was letting volleyball consume my life.

The next week was filled with uncertainties. I had surgery to remove the cancer and some lymph nodes. The severity of the melanoma would not be determined until the biopsy reports came back.

During this long week of uncertainty, I found tremendous peace in knowing that God was in control. Philippians 4:6–7, which have become my favorite verses, gave me God's amazing comfort. It says, "Do not be anxious about anything, but in everything, by prayer and petition, with thanksgiving, present your requests to God. And the peace of God, . . . will guard your hearts."

Through God's grace, I received His peace, I knew He was in control and He carried me through. My surgery was a success! The cancer was contained, and it had not spread. Three weeks later and all stitched up, I was able to help my team qualify for the 2000 Olympics. I learned to rely more on God through this trying experience and always put Him first.

—*Val Kemper, former member, US national volleyball team*

GAME PLAN

What are you facing that has you frightened or uncertain? Have you begun to give that to God in prayer?

From the Playbook:

Read Philippians 4:4–9.

76

BORN-AGAIN CHAMPIONS

"Run in such a way as to get the prize." 1 CORINTHIANS 9:24

On this society of competitiveness and winning at all cost, it is a common misperception that Christians are too nice to be good athletes. I often hear new believers struggling with how to be competitive as a Christian. Yes, your perspective on sports will change once you are born again, but it should not prevent you from being a champion. In fact, it should help you!

Once you realize that winning is not the most important thing, and anything less is a failure, it takes the pressure off. Getting bogged down in the pressures of performance and results is the fall of many athletes. Many of the factors that go into the end-result are out of your control.

What *is* in your control is doing everything to the best of your ability. Keeping your eyes on Christ and focusing on pleasing Him—that's running the race to get the *real* prize.

God gave us talents so we could use them to glorify Him. He wants us to be awesome! He blesses us so that we can bless other people and bring glory to Him. We need to recognize the gifts He gave us and use them for His will, knowing that they are from the Lord, our maker.

All athletes want to win, and that is okay. But remember that sometimes it is not part of His master plan for us to win the game on earth. But He wants us to compete as if we are striving for the ultimate prize—eternity!

—*Jenny Boucek, coach, WNBA*

GAME PLAN

Is there anything in your life that you think is a specific skill or knowledge or ability God gave you to serve Him? How have you used that skill in the past week to glorify God?

From the Playbook:

Read 1 Corinthians 9:19–27.

LOOKING FOR JOY IN THE RIGHT PLACE

"When anxiety was great within me, your consolation brought joy to my soul." PSALM 94:19

One night during my rookie year with the Minnesota Lynx, we played in Madison Square Garden against the New York Liberty in front of 14,000 people. The game was close, and the lead seesawed back and forth.

As the game wound down to the final moments, we were behind by just two points, and I was still on the floor. Suddenly, I found the ball in my hands with less than 10 seconds to go. I drove to the basket and got fouled with 6 seconds left. Talk about unexpected! Here I was at the free throw line with our team's last chance to tie the game as 14,000 people screamed at me. And trust me, they weren't yelling encouragement.

I stepped to the line and shot the ball—then watched in horror as it missed the rim, the backboard, and the net. I was a pro basketball player who had been playing ball for twelve years, and I had air-balled the easiest shot in the game.

We had a chance at an upset, and I blew it. I felt worthless. I had let down the team, the coaches, the fans, and myself.

I learned a valuable lesson through this experience. I had allowed my desire to be a successful athlete overrun my desire to be a child of God—pleasing in His sight. I had fallen into the trap of believing that my identity and self-worth depended on how well I performed on the court. That's just not true.

Because of Calvary, my salvation is secure. My security is in Christ. Sure the sting of choking in crunch time was no fun, but it was a good reminder that my performance is not where my true joy comes from. My joy is found in Jesus—the delight of my soul.

—*Erin Buescher Perperoglu, former WNBA guard*

GAME PLAN

What error have you made recently that made you forget that your worth is in Jesus, not in your performance? What can you learn from Erin's experience?

From the Playbook:

Read Philippians 2:1–18.

HOLD ON!

"You need to persevere." HEBREWS **10:36**

Imagine what it would be like to be an Olympian, proudly representing your country at the Opening Ceremonies—smiling and waving to more than 100,000 people as they cheer for you.

Perhaps you would even finish in the Top Three and receive a gold, silver, or bronze medal.

Picturing yourself as a famous Olympic athlete can be fun, and if you're an athlete it can motivate you to work hard. No matter how lofty your goal, though, things come up that cause you to feel like quitting.

But even the excitement of the goal is not always enough to keep you going. LaVonna Floreal, 1992 100-meter hurdles Olympic silver medalist, remembers what it was like to pursue Olympic dreams when she felt like giving up. To block distractions, she would focus on a target and work everything else around that mark. In her words, "it's like having a circle with a point in the middle that you can always see unless you turn your back away from it."

Endurance is perseverance. It is pressing on when you want to stop because of obstacles, trials, or ridicule. LaVonna learned how to endure hardships as an athlete in order to reach her goal. Still today, she applies the disciplines she learned as an athlete to her Christian walk and her goal of glorifying God.

Each day we face temptations and obstacles that can cause us to sin or falter in our walk of faith. Yet as a successful athlete continues to persevere, so should we. "Let us hold unswervingly to the hope we profess," the author of Hebrews says (10:23). When we do that, nothing can stop us from doing what God wants us to do.

—*Roxanne Robbins*

GAME PLAN

Today, list three worthy goals and three things you need to do to reach those goals. Ask God to help you stay disciplined so you can finish the task and bring Him glory in the process.

From the Playbook:
Read Hebrews 10.

LOOK BEHIND THE CLOUDS

"The Lord God is a sun and shield; the Lord bestows favor and honor." PSALM 84:11

After flying quite a bit one summer while playing for the Washington Freedom in the Women's United Soccer Association, I was reminded of the sovereignty of God over and over again.

As always I grabbed a window seat—they are the best seats. There's just something about being up in that sky, gazing out the window, and seeing God's splendor. The plane had just taken off. I turned to look out the window. It was another dreary, rainy day. But as we climbed to a greater altitude, we were soon breaking through the gray clouds. To my amazement, my eyes were suddenly fixed on a brilliant sunrise.

On other flights, I would glance out the window and I wouldn't be able to see anything. There would just be the dreary clouds of a lingering storm. It was during those times that I had to remind myself of the beauty I had seen earlier. A blue sky really was out there, even though I couldn't see it at that moment.

God will take you through tough times, but He will always bring you back to the realization of His sovereignty and His care for you. There is always a blue sky.

I have learned that if God is going to teach you something He is going to "live you through it." At the end of trying times, whether it was a loss, an injury, or another struggle, I became stronger knowing I had survived. I kept my sites on what I knew to be true.

When you look out the window of a plane, you may see clouds and rain—but remember what that blue sky looks like. The sun is still shining, even if you can't see its rays. Comfort, peace, and confidence will rest in your heart.

—*Amanda Cromwell, college soccer coach*

GAME PLAN

What clouds are blocking your view of God's provision and love? How can your trust in God help you see past them?

From the Playbook:
Read Psalm 84:10–12.

RIDING THE WAVES

"But when he asks, he must believe and not doubt." JAMES 1:6

Margo Oberg is a five-time world champion surfer who lives and rides the water in Hawaii. She's had some serious surf encounters, but none quite as scary as the time she almost "bought it" when she was 16. It all began after Margo wiped out on a humongous wave.

Here are Margo's own words: "Below the wave it looks like a mini-tornado, and you spin around and then usually come up. But sometimes there's so much pressure that you grope for the top and there's no way up."

That's what happened on this not-so-sweet-16 occasion.

Panic set in, and Margo started swimming for the surface—not realizing that she was actually heading straight down. She became delirious and nearly blacked out.

Miraculously (she believes God brought her up), her motionless body began to rise to the surface like a cork. She was able to flounder onto shore.

Margo wouldn't have that panic problem today. She's ridden the waves long enough to relax and not freak out when a wave turns her upside down.

You get a lot of stuff thrown at you every day—new ideas, odd philosophies, touchy emotional issues. Do you sometimes feel like a wave being driven by the wind? Do you feel as if you're swimming down instead of up?

Hold tightly to your faith in Christ. Pray to Him. Acknowledge that He "does not change like shifting shadows" (James 1:17). The more you do, the easier it is to avoid getting drowned with strange ideas.

Surf's up!

GAME PLAN

What do you need to do to become better at recognizing and avoiding wrong "waves"?

—*Tom Felten*

From the Playbook:
Read James 1:1–18.

LEAN ON GOD

"In all your ways acknowledge him." PROVERBS 3:6

As a child, Olympian Wilma Rudolph suffered through polio, double pneumonia, and scarlet fever, which caused her to lose the use of her left leg. From the age of six she wore a brace. A doctor told Wilma's mother that rubbing her daughter's leg might help. So every day Wilma received four leg-rubs from her brothers, sisters, and mother. Eventually she graduated from a brace to an orthopedic shoe, and she joined her brothers playing basketball whenever she could.

One day, Wilma's mother returned home and found her daughter playing basketball without her brace. Five years later, Wilma had developed into a star runner and at age sixteen qualified for the US Olympic team. She went on to win three gold medals in 1960—in the 100- and 200-meter dashes and the 4 x 100 meter relay.

Wilma refused to lean on the understanding that she was crippled. As a result she went on to greatness.

Proverbs 3:5–6 says, "Trust in the Lord with all your heart and lean not on your own understanding; in all your ways acknowledge him, and he will make your paths straight." When you face a challenge, meditate on this verse. Write down your understanding of your situation and consider whether you're leaning on it. One way to tell if you're leaning on your understanding is by the actions you're taking or paralysis you're experiencing as a result.

For example, you might be afraid to go on an overseas mission trip. It's okay to be cautious, but instead of leaning on the unknown as you make decisions, you need to acknowledge God with your concerns. Learn to lean on God, and watch things really take off.

—*Roxanne Robbins*

GAME PLAN

As you make decisions today, big or small, ask, "Am I trusting myself, or am I trusting God completely?"

From the Playbook:

Read Proverbs 3.

CAN YOU OUTGIVE GOD?

"Bring the whole tithe into the storehouse." Malachi 3:10

In my first year as a professional golfer, my church had voiced a need for a family that urgently needed financial help. I felt a nudging to contribute to the benevolent fund, but I was unsure of the amount I should commit. After some thought and prayer, I decided I would give 10 percent of my next check to the fund on top of my regular tithe. Considering that the biggest check in my professional career until then was $2,000, I didn't think much of it.

In the very next tournament I played, I finished tied for second place and took home the biggest check of my career—$4,000. Now I was in a little bit of a dilemma. I was expecting to give around $200 to this fund, but now 10 percent would mean I would have to double that.

To make my decision even more difficult, I had not told anyone about my vow. Furthermore, I was sure that whatever I did contribute would have been received with thanksgiving. I decided to write the check for $400 and send it off immediately—before I could have second thoughts. As I was leaving for the next tournament, the family I was staying with for the week put a card in my car just before I pulled out.

Once I arrived at my next destination, I opened the card and found $500 in cash along with several pre-paid calling cards. They had no idea of my commitment to God, but God knew.

You can never outgive God. This does not mean that in order for God to bless you, you have to give money to the church. It's not about us—it's about Him. He wants us to be faithful in the stewardship of the resources He gives us—and to honor our commitments.

—*Siew-Ai Lim, former LPGA golfer*

> **GAME PLAN**
>
> What about this idea of tithing? Is it a habit in your life? Could it be possible that it is the least God expects of us?

From the Playbook:
Read Leviticus 27 and Malachi 3.
Consider how those Old Testament standards
should fit into your world today.

WHEN GOD ASKS THE QUESTIONS

"We are hard pressed on every side, but not crushed;
perplexed, but not in despair; persecuted, but not abandoned;
struck down, but not destroyed." 2 CORINTHIANS 4:8

While playing with the Washington Freedom in the Women's United Soccer Association, I tried to bring my best to everything I did. That was my approach in every game, every practice, every chapel, and every encounter with family and friends.

You never know when it's going to be your last day at the stadium. This was a concept I learned back in 1996.

That year I tore my ACL 6 months before the Olympics. I questioned God when that happened. I wanted to know: "Why did You allow this to happen? Why do I have to go through this right now? Why did it turn out this way?"

You know what happened next? I came to my senses and realized that God asks us questions also. He asks, "Why did you ignore Me this morning? Why don't you trust Me? Why don't you spend time with Me? Why can't you be satisfied with just Me?"

There were times during the summer of 2001 when I felt a bit like Play-Doh. I was being pushed and pulled, squeezed and pounded in all different directions, in all areas of my life. The reality of this is that although the Play-Doh goes through all these changes, it never loses its consistency, it never loses its toughness, and it never loses its identity. It is still Play-Doh.

Same thing with us. We may go through some trials, some struggles, but it doesn't change who we are in Christ. We still have our identity in Christ. We can still trust Him.

I had to learn to trust Him, be satisfied with Him, and spend quality time with Him. That is how I dig in and stay focused. God gets me through the pushes and pulls, and that allows me to bring my best to every situation.

—*Amanda Cromwell, college soccer coach*

GAME PLAN

What are some of the questions you sometimes ask God? What are the answers He wants from you?

From the Playbook:
Read 2 Corinthians 4:8–9.

LOSING ON A WINNING TEAM

"He who has begun a good work in you will carry it on to completion until the day of Christ Jesus." PHILIPPIANS 1:6

Renee was only in high school, but she displayed Olympic potential. One of the fastest 200-meter runners in the US, the only thing holding her back was that she never took responsibility for her God-given talent—she was extremely lazy. Consequently, she did not develop the confidence she needed.

The day came when Renee's team competed at the US National Track & Field Championships. The team qualified to run in the 800-meter medley finals. She would be running the third leg—200 meters. Waiting to run the final 400 meters was a runner who held the 400-meter world record. If Renee could hand off the baton in second place, the anchor runner could bring home a victory.

The gun fired and everything was going perfectly when Renee took the baton in third place. As the fourth runner waited for the handoff, she figured Renee would pull them up to second, and she would go after first place. Poised to receive the baton, she watched helplessly as one runner after another went past. The whole field went by before she saw Renee slowly coming off the curve, holding her side.

She knew that Renee had decided not to run, and she was faking an injury. When the pressure was on, Renee had no confidence. She hadn't trained to win. Surprisingly, the team pulled out a victory, but as the others celebrated, Renee became the loser on a winning team.

God gives all of us unique gifts and talents. But just like Renee, if we don't develop them, we may become losers among winners. Colossians 3:23 tells us to do everything "heartily, as to the Lord" (NKJV). When we develop our gifts and talents to glorify Him, victory is ours. We are never losers in the eyes of Jesus.   —*Madeline Mims, Olympic medalist, track*

GAME PLAN

"Father, I repent of any slothfulness in my life that will cause me to lose out on experiencing the blessings You have for me. My hope and confidence are in You, my beloved Creator and God. I praise You with my life."

From the Playbook:
Read Psalm 27.

NEED A SHOWER?

"Do not conform any longer to the pattern of this world, but be transformed by the renewing of your mind." ROMANS 12:2

After a game or a match we feel pretty grimy, don't we? We are in dire need of a shower with lots of soap!

Well, think about all the dirt in the world from a spiritual standpoint. Every day we are confronted by sin around us. We see it, smell it, and sense it even from afar. The ability to detect sin is a trait our heavenly Father gave us when we became His. As we live in this world, we have to battle the dirt on a daily basis.

Should we remain grimy? Not at all. Just as we take a shower physically to remove the dirt of our athletic competition, we need a spiritual shower to remove the grime of life. Daily we need to come to the Father and cleanse our heart and mind. We need to repent and be washed clean. It's a privilege we have as a child of God—free forgiveness.

As we are cleansed, we then need to fill our minds with God and His truth! If we don't, then the dirt we picked up from the world filters into our mind.

Where do we dwell? Where do our minds dwell? Psalm 119:11 says, "I have hidden your word in my heart that I might not sin against you." Philippians 4:7 says, "The peace of God, which transcends all understanding, will guard your hearts and your minds in Christ Jesus."

With all the spiritual dirt in the locker room, on the playing field, and in the hotel rooms—cover your hearts, renew your minds, and dwell on God and His precious truth! Be clean.

—*Kim Braatz-Voisard, former pro baseball player*

GAME PLAN

What grime is most likely to stick to you? Which of the world's sinful offerings affects you the most? Spend some time asking God to clean those things off you and protect you.

From the Playbook:

Read Psalm 51, which is David's plea for forgiveness when he got himself filthy with sin.

HOW TO GET UP WHEN YOU'RE DOWN

"Give, and it will be given to you." LUKE 6:38

Do you ever feel a little down? As athletes, we go through a lot of intense emotions. Our confidence ebbs and flows. How do you handle the down times? Do you feel sorry for yourself? Do you let excuses justify your behavior? Do you let your problems affect the whole team?

When you find yourself in a bad mood, the best way to get out of the funk is to lift other people up. Instead of moping in practice and bringing negative energy around the team, make an extra effort to cheer for your teammates and give them compliments. If you do, you will not only keep from letting your selfish issues affect the team, but you will also feel better. God will honor that, and He will give you an unexplainable joy.

Give and you will receive. Give good energy and you will get good energy. Give negative energy and that is what you will get.

Don't depend on others to make you happy. You are in control of your moods and how you handle circumstances. Sometimes you may not feel like being in a good mood, but if you fake it, you will start to feel it. And in the meantime, you may just lift someone else up and brighten his day.

Helping others is one of the best remedies for the blues. Don't give to get, because God knows your heart. But if you give with a pure heart, you will be sure to receive!

—*Jenny Boucek, coach, WNBA*

GAME PLAN

Whose day can I brighten today? Who needs that extra touch of kindness?

From the Playbook:
Read Proverbs 11:23–31.

THE EYES OF A SPY

"I call to the Lord, who is worthy of praise, and I am saved from my enemies." PSALM **18:3**

For a few weeks every summer, my assistant coaches and I go out recruiting in gymnasiums nationwide. You could say that we're "spying on" the great players. Since many of them have incredible physical talent, our job is to see through to their character. We want to know who they are in times of adversity and how they approach the game.

Have you ever read in the Bible about Joshua, Caleb, and the twelve spies? It's a captivating story that begins when twelve leaders are selected to spy out the Promised Land and report back to their people, the Israelites. What they saw was an abundance of food, a fertile land "flowing with milk and honey," just what God had promised them. But unexpectedly, they also saw fortified cities and extremely large men like giants. So ten of the spies allowed fear into their hearts and convinced the Israelites that there was no hope in trusting God. But two men stood strong and insisted that there was hope, that God was true to His word. They saw through the unexpected obstacles to the truth of God's promise.

Often, I watch players to see how they react when unexpected things happen. What about us? How do we respond when life throws a curve at us? Do we tremble with fear? Do we stand strong in what we believe even when we're standing alone?

Unbelief looks at obstacles that stand in the way; faith looks at the God who is able to overcome those obstacles. The eyes of a good spy see God in every situation.

—*Sue Semrau, women's college basketball coach*

GAME PLAN

What obstacles are standing in your way today? Obstacles that prevent you from trusting God completely?

From the Playbook:
Read Numbers 13.

88

REALIGNED PRIORITIES

"There are different kinds of gifts, but the same Spirit."
1 Corinthians 12:4

By the time I was a seventh grader, I knew the Lord had blessed me with the gift of speed. I decided to make the most of my gift. I committed myself to the game of basketball.

By following this work ethic, I made it to the WNBA. I was a member of the Utah Starzz and living my dream. Then lightning struck! I was cut by the Starzz midway through my second season. I was devastated. I felt as if I had failed.

Reflecting on that time, I realize I didn't fail in my effort. I had worked hard and used the gifts God had blessed me with as much as I could. Where I failed, however, was in my priorities. I had been using my gifts for my personal glory and determining my success and failure based upon society's standards. What should have mattered was how I used my talent for God's glory, and I hadn't done that. God, however, knew how to help me realign my priorities.

I had been at home in Boise, Idaho, for two weeks when I received a call to play for the Cleveland Rockers. Upon arriving in Cleveland, I went to chapel with our chaplain, Alice Simpson, before my first game. She and one other Rockers player were the only other two in attendance. I wondered why God would take me away from Utah, where I had been surrounded by other Christians, and place me among so many non-believers.

GAME PLAN

Is God pointing you in a direction that feels uncomfortable? Could it be that He has some grand things in store for you if you would follow Him?

I did not then know God's intentions. But a short year after my arrival in Cleveland, seven of the eleven players on my team were attending chapels regularly. Teammates were reading devotionals on airplanes. I have used this special gift and brought non-believers to Christ. This, to me, has been well worth the sorrow I faced for such a short time and has also been the best victory I could ever win.

—*Tricia Binford, former WNBA guard*

From the Playbook:
Read 1 Corinthians 12.

QUIT COMPLAINING ...
START THANKING

"Give thanks in all circumstances." 1 THESSALONIANS 5:18

NASCAR Craftsman Truck Series driver Kelly Sutton has overcome multiple challenges to become one of the few women to excel in the male-dominated sport. And the obstacles have not all been gender related. Sutton has also had to jump extraordinary physical hurdles because she has Multiple Sclerosis (MS).

Sutton, the only NASCAR driver in history to race with MS, told *Sports Spectrum* writer Jim Gibbs, "I like challenges, and MS is just a part of my life. It's like a bump in the road or a bump on the racetrack, and you've got to find ways to get over it.

"I've just incorporated it all into my daily routine," she says, "which is nothing really special. I just eat healthy foods and work out. In the off-season, I work with a trainer and try to maintain good health throughout the year. I do like to swim, and I try to do that as much as I can. But I also train with weights. Not so much to build muscles but to build endurance in the muscles."

Sutton doesn't complain about her afflictions. Instead she embraces the opportunity to glorify God by giving thanks for what she can do. She lives out 1 Thessalonians 5:16–18, which says, "Be joyful always; pray continually; give thanks in all circumstances, for this is God's will for you in Christ Jesus."

If you feel that you've been a complainer recently, today choose instead to thank God and entrust your future to Him.

—*Roxanne Robbins*

GAME PLAN

Think about a person who overcame physical setbacks to excel in a sport. Take a few minutes to talk to this person about the situation. What can you learn from his or her example?

From the Playbook:
Read 1 Thessalonians 5:12–28.

WHO GETS THE FOCUS?

"Set your minds on things above, not on earthly things."
COLOSSIANS 3:2

It was the 1968 Olympic Games in Mexico City, and I was waiting to go out to the track to run my first round in the women's 800-meter race. A reporter from my hometown had somehow made it through security. "Hi, Madeline. Everyone back home sends good wishes to you. We're real proud of you and surprised at what you've accomplished here."

I was puzzled. I had been the best female 800-meter runner in the world for the last two years. What was so surprising about my competing at the Olympic Games?

He continued, "Madeline, we're glad you've made it this far, but do you think you will make it?" The sting of his words numbed my mind. What did he mean? I hadn't considered the idea that I wouldn't make it, whatever IT was.

Before he could finish his sentence, I sharply turned, looked him in the eye, and said, "I have learned that everybody here has come to win, and I'm no different. So you just watch me."

As I walked away I began to think about what the reporter said. I had worked hard to get to this place in my life, yet I was now fighting doubt and fear.

I prayed, and God reminded me that I was beautifully and wonderfully made. Confidence again soared through my being as I remembered that my Creator had made me an athlete to glorify Him. I began to focus on paying my vows to the Lord in the presence of all His people. I won my heat, my semi-finals, and then the finals for the gold medal.

If we focus our attention on the purpose God intended for our lives, we will never lose focus of who we are, and the reason we do what we do.
—*Madeline Mims, Olympic medalist, track*

GAME PLAN

"Father, may I always bring glory to You by being what You have made me to be. You have blessed my life to be a blessing to others. I will only become what You have purposed me to be, for Your workmanship on my life is enough in Christ Jesus."

From the Playbook:
Read: Psalms 139; 116; and 117.

WHAT HAS YOUR ATTENTION?

"But you didn't pay a bit of attention to me, Jacob. You so quickly tired of me, Israel." ISAIAH 43:22 (THE MESSAGE)

It was the 2004 US Open women's quarterfinals. Crowds gathered to watch tennis champions Svetlana Kuznetsova and Nadia Petrova play match after match, competing at the top of their game.

And then came the rain. What was left of Hurricane Frances washed over the National Tennis Center in Flushing Meadows, New York, suspending games and rerouting players to different courts. Kuznetsova and Petrova were assigned to Court 11—the outside venue, where there were, by actual count, only thirteen people in the stands. The attention of fair-weather tennis fans had quickly been diverted.

Scripture itself is saturated with stories of people who too easily stopped paying attention to what they were supposed to be watching. Samson, Esau, Saul, Solomon, and even King David all lost sight of God. They turned their attention to other things. God pleaded with the people of Israel. "'Return, faithless Israel,' ... 'I will frown on you no longer, for I am merciful'" (Jeremiah 3:12). Despite their faintheartedness, God was still devoted to saving His people.

Are you easily diverted by life's circumstances? Could you be a fair-weather fan when it comes to following Jesus? Although following God may sometimes feel unpopular, too hard to pursue, or even somewhat like sitting in the rain, the pursuit is still worth it! When you do get distracted, remember that God is still committed to you. Turn your attention back to Him today.

—Molly Ramseyer

GAME PLAN

What activities in your life distract you from focusing on Jesus? Decide today to spend ten more minutes with Jesus instead of serving that "distraction."

From the Playbook:
Read 2 Samuel 11:1–27. Read about David's distraction.

DON'T FORGET THE SMALL THINGS

"I thank my God every time I remember you." PHILIPPIANS 1:3

It was Saturday afternoon, and I just hung up the phone with Mom. I asked her to tell me she loved me, something I had never had to do before. But, something in my spirit prompted me to make sure I heard her say, "I love you, Honey."

Mom was in her ninth month of battling melanoma cancer, and her body was wearing out rapidly. I called home every day to talk with her. As the days passed, the conversations became shorter and shorter.

The day after my perplexing conversation, I received a call from home. It was my sister telling me that mom had died a few hours earlier. I was stunned, speechless and paralyzed.

In my state of shock, I thought back to that conversation the day prior. God knew that I needed to hear those words one more time. He created a memory that I can hold on to during the times when I miss mom and I long to pick up the phone and just say, "Hello."

It's easy to forget to thank God for the blessings He's given me in my life. But the one gift I will continue to thank Him for is the remembrance of my mother's last words to me.

It may seem like a small thing, but it'll stick with me for years and years to come.

Remember to "Devote yourselves to prayer, being watchful and thankful" (Colossians 4:2). And thank God for the small things.

—*Tracy Hanson, former LPGA golfer*

GAME PLAN

Write down five "small" things you were thankful for this past week. Spend time in prayer talking to God and thanking Him for these blessings.

From the Playbook:

Read Psalm 136 and think about the many things for which we can praise God.

WHAT IS GOD'S PLAN?

"'For I know the plans I have for you,' declares the Lord."
JEREMIAH **29:11**

After training with the USA National Volleyball team for almost four years, the big day finally arrived. The final cut for the 2000 Olympic team was about to happen. I felt confident. My fitness level was at its peak. My dream was about to come true.

There were 15 girls in the room as the head coach revealed which 12 players would travel to Sydney for the 2000 Olympics. He listed the names and left the room.

I thought there was a mistake. Where was my name? Perhaps he left it off accidentally. I counted the names. There were 12 names, and Val Sterk was not listed. How could this be? Some of the players on the list had been with the team for only a couple months; I had been there for years! My heart was broken; my dreams, crushed. Suddenly, the thousands of hours in the gym, the sweat, the tears—it all became meaningless.

My dream to play volleyball in the Olympics was shattered. Why had God put me through this for four years just to be cut at the very end? I spent a long time in prayer, and finally I began to realize that sometimes our plans don't match God's plan. Proverbs 19:21 says, "Many are the plans in a man's heart, but it is the Lord's purpose that prevails."

The day I was cut from the Olympic team was also the day I had my first date with Olympic triathlete Hunter Kemper. Our relationship developed quickly, and I was given the opportunity to travel with his family to Sydney to support him and my volleyball teammates at the Olympics.

That disappointing day in 2000 had a bright ending. Three years later, I would marry the man of my dreams, Hunter Kemper. Now I know why God had me at the Olympic Training Center all those years. God's plan truly is the best.

—*Val Kemper, former member, US national volleyball team*

GAME PLAN

Where do you think God's plan has gone awry? Have you prayed and asked God to reveal what He is doing?

From the Playbook:
Read Jeremiah 29:4–13.

HANG ON FOR THE RIDE OF YOUR LIFE

"Where the Spirit of the Lord is, there is freedom."
2 CORINTHIANS 3:17

If I had my choice of what to do on a hot summer day, I'd go out on a beautiful lake and water-ski. It's one of my all-time favorite activities. If you've ever water-skied, you can imagine how it relates to being a follower of Jesus Christ.

In water-skiing, simply getting up on the skis is a tremendous feat. It's a matter of having a good stance and letting the boat do the work. Similarly, trusting Christ to be our Master can be a very difficult choice, because pride, in its various forms, throws us off balance. But when we choose Christ, we put ourselves in position to receive His free gift of salvation, and the Holy Spirit does the work of changing us on the inside and out.

Once you get up on the skis, the ride is almost effortless. In fact, there is an area behind the boat, called the wake, which fans out, and if you ski straight and stay within this area, the ride is smooth and few waves will trouble you. Likewise, many believers stay in their comfortable place spiritually. They shy away from challenges and risks for fear of making mistakes or looking silly. But Christ calls us to experience life to the fullest. "Where the Spirit of the Lord is, there is freedom" (2 Corinthians 3:17). He wants us to get out of the wake, to slalom the waters of life with enthusiasm.

We need to trust God. After all, He's driving.

—*Sue Semrau, college women's basketball coach*

GAME PLAN

What are three non-comfort zone things you think God wants you to do this week? Keep track of them and keep yourself accountable to complete them.

From the Playbook:

Read Acts 21 for an example of how Paul kept leaving his comfort zone to reach people.

WHY SPORTS?

"Be conformed to the likeness of his Son." ROMANS **8:29**

Sports—why do people play them? Why do people follow them with such fervor? What is the motive?

Athletes have a multitude of reasons for playing sports—it could be because they are good at it, they need a college scholarship, they want to please their parents, they like to compete, or they like recognition. Sports fans might follow sports because games are a form of recreation, they love the sport, they live vicariously through their favorite athlete, or because they love the thrill of winning and losing.

I believe sports are a microcosm of life. All of the elements of life are condensed into a few months of high-intensity growth. Athletes are confronted with physical, mental, and emotional strain. They have to persevere under trial, to discipline themselves, to recover from failure and defeat—and to do it all with grace. We often forget that God allows us to participate in sports to show us who we are and how much we need Him.

God is more concerned with who we become as we play sports than what the score of the game is. And for some people, sports are the best way to learn about life.

Even the apostle Paul used sports. He reminded us that life is like running a race and that we are to run in such a way as to get the prize. We are to have purpose and discipline as we progress spiritually. For the Christian, playing sports is another tool God can use to teach us how to live a holy life.

—*Molly Ramseyer*

GAME PLAN

Why are you interested in sports? Is your motive tied to this world and its pleasures or does it have eternal significance?

From the Playbook:
Read 1 Corinthians 9:24–27.

COMPETITIVE AND CONTENT?

"I have learned to be content whatever the circumstances."
PHILIPPIANS 4:11

Contentment for a competitive athlete seems like a contradiction. Most athletes are encouraged by coaches to strive only toward winning. The development of a winning attitude is paramount in attaining great success. Often any hint of a negative attitude is a sure sign of defeat. Because of this, many are faced with winning at all costs.

As an athlete, I struggled with being satisfied in any situation. The truth is . . . I wanted to win! Losing was not an option for me. Consequently, I would put a lot of pressure on myself if I lost a race. This is not difficult to do in an individual sport such as track and field. Your sole reliance is not on a team, but on yourself. Not until I learned this principle of contentment did I truly succeed as an athlete.

One example occurred during my return to competition after a 14-month absence from the sport. Prior to this point in my career, winning and losing was the focus of my heart. Like many, I found my self-worth in what I accomplished on the track. Slowly, I became dissatisfied if I didn't accomplish my goals. After my layoff from competition, the Lord began to mold my heart toward satisfaction in Him. His plan for my life began to unfold as I looked toward His face. Because of this new focus, He graciously gave me my heart's desire of an Olympic medal.

Although I still struggle with contentment in my life, I forever have a reminder of His power, which is available when my focal point is on Him.
—*LaVonna Martin-Floreal, Olympic silver medalist, track*

GAME PLAN

What are three areas of your life for which you lack contentment? What do you try to do to find the joy you so much desire? How often do you include God in your search for contentment?

From the Playbook:
Read 1 Timothy 6:6–10.

THE BEST IS YET TO COME

"He who began a good work in you will carry it on."
PHILIPPIANS 1:6

Madeline Manning Mims was a member of four Summer Olympic teams. In 1968 she won gold in the women's 800 meters, setting Olympic, American, and world records. She was the first American woman to break the 2-minute barrier in the 800 meters.

Today Madeline serves as an official chaplain for professional and Olympic track athletes. Frequently she shares the value Philippians 1:6 has had in her life. It says, "Being confident of this, that he who began a good work in you will carry it on to completion until the day of Christ Jesus."

GAME PLAN

How has God changed your life and heart this past year? Thank Him in advance for the good work He will complete in your life.

Speaking of this verse, Madeline says, "This Scripture has been an encouragement to me during my active athletics and in the everyday race of life. My confidence is not based on my talents, gifts, or hard work alone, but on what God has done for me, to me, in me, and through me. When I meditate on the fact that what He has started in me is a good work that is constantly being processed into a finished work, I am encouraged to keep obeying His will for my life.

" 'He's not finished with me yet' and 'The best is yet to come' are ideals that I trust as I anticipate my future. It helps me to know that no matter how short I may fall of His glory, God will never give up on me. This knowledge gives me confidence."

How exciting that is—to live with the anticipation that God is not finished and that He has even greater things in mind for us.

—*Roxanne Robbins*

From the Playbook:
Read Philippians 1:3–11.

ALONE TIME

"He went up . . . by himself to pray." MATTHEW 14:23

ave you ever dreamed of cracking a walk-off three-run homer in the bottom of the ninth inning to send your team home happy? How about draining the game-winning three-pointer with thousands of fans watching?

What athlete hasn't spent some time dreaming about such scenarios?

In order to put yourself in the hero position, you've got to do something first—every athlete has to put in some "alone" time.

Whether you're working on dribbling drills or shooting free throws, you've got to put in some significant time—just you and your "rock." (Or your baseball bat, football, or hockey stick.)

Every athlete has to work hard to improve his or her skills and to hone his or her game. If you think for a minute that you can improve your play without individual work—drills, conditioning, shooting—you're in for a big surprise! Sure, practices and scrimmages are a lot more fun. (You're actually competing against someone.) But the real improvement and growth comes from individual practice time.

A consistent walk of faith is similar. In order to live out your Christian faith, you've got to put in some alone time with God. That's where your faith is nurtured and developed.

Our Lord Jesus revealed the importance of this alone time with God in Matthew 14 when He went to a mountainside to pray by Himself.

Yes, practicing your faith among friends is important, but so is developing and nurturing it—alone.

—*Rob Bentz*

GAME PLAN

Practice the following prayer exercise. Spend 20 minutes of your time in prayer. Use the first 5 minutes to praise God for who He is and for His amazing attributes. Use the next 5 minutes to thank Him for specific blessings in your life. Use the next 5 to pray for specific needs and requests. Then take the final 5 minutes to be still before God and listen.

From the Playbook:
Read Matthew 14:13–21.

IT'S ALL ABOUT . . . OTHERS

"Love never fails." 1 CORINTHIANS 13:8

"I have to look out for my own interests. I have to do what's best for me. If I don't look out for myself, no one else will." How many times have we heard those words from a free-agent athlete who has made more than enough money to last most people a couple of lifetimes? We've almost come to expect this "me-centered" approach to life, and not just from athletes. I think we've all bought into looking at life selfishly more than we'd like to admit.

Which is what makes the "others-centered" nature of what Esther Kim did at the US Olympic Taekwondo Trials in Colorado Springs so exceptional. At the start of the flyweight final match, Esther conceded, allowing her best friend and training partner, Kay Poe, to win. Kay, top ranked in the world, had injured her left knee in the semifinal and could barely stand up. "If we clashed hard enough, her knee might have been permanently injured," Esther said. Esther Kim forfeited a spot on the US Olympic taekwondo team so her friend could go to the 2000 Games in Sydney. She later commented, "I wasn't throwing my dreams away; I was handing them to Kay."

In John 13 Jesus said that His followers could be identified by the way they loved each other. He said, "Love one another. As I have loved you, so you must love one another. By this all men will know that you are my disciples, if you love one another" (vv. 34–35).

Have you done any "others-centered" loving lately? It's a great way to let friends and loved ones know that you are a follower of Christ.

—*Brian Hettinga*

GAME PLAN

Do a random act of kindness for someone today. Thinking of a kindness and doing it will be a step toward becoming an "others-centered" representative of Jesus Christ.

From the Playbook:

Read about love in 1 Corinthians 13.

THE SILENT SEASON

"Be prepared in season and out of season." 2 Timothy 4:2

Preseason.

It's weight training, strength training, speed training. It's drills, plyometrics, nutrition.

It's going to the camps for exposure, to the gym for conditioning, and to Foot Locker for the new shoes.

Preseason is not just about getting ready for a new start; it is also about putting last season behind you. And the grueling thing about preseason is that there aren't any fans. There is no one watching to see if you went hard your last 10 minutes or if you finished each set. There is no one cheering you on as you complete each workout. But after the time of preparation, there will come a time when it will all pay off.

Preseason is like spiritual life. The apostle Paul reminds us to "forget what is behind and strain toward what is ahead" (Philippians 3:13). No matter what your "last season" looked like spiritually, you have to set it aside and strive toward a life of faith and obedience. Peter reminds us to always be prepared to give an answer for the hope that we have (1 Peter 3:15). Always be in "spiritual shape" to tell others about what Christ has done in your life. Paul again challenges us to "be prepared in season and out of season," to preach the Word and instruct others (2 Timothy 4:2).

> **GAME PLAN**
>
> Are you "in shape" spiritually? What is holding you back? Pray and ask God for discipline and strength. Then whip your spiritual self into shape.

Spiritual exercise is very grueling, and often no one will notice the time you spend behind closed doors with your Savior. No one is counting; no one is cheering. But a time is coming when preseason will be over, the game will be on, and "your reward will be great" (Luke 6:35).

—*Molly Ramseyer*

From the Playbook:
Read Philippians 3:12–4:1.

OVERCOMING A BAD START

"They took him and threw him into the cistern." GENESIS 37:24

When Wilma Rudolph was four years old, she got a bad case of scarlet fever, and she lost the use of her left leg. She didn't learn to walk again until she was seven years old.

In 1960, this same determined young woman, now twenty years old, won three gold medals at the Summer Olympic Games—in running events. She overcame a slow start in life and became a champion.

Old Testament hero Joseph had some obstacles too. Although his were not physical like Wilma's, they were huge roadblocks.

As a boy reared in a blended family, he was favored by his father and hated by his jealous half-brothers. They thought they got rid of him by selling him into slavery. And when he got to Egypt, he was falsely accused of trying to seduce his master's wife and thrown into prison.

Yet Joseph became a model of courage and dependence on God. Despite many setbacks, he rose to become governor of Egypt. Under God's providence he became the "savior" of his family—including those very brothers who had treated him so cruelly.

Perhaps you're off to a bad start spiritually. Maybe you've made some bad choices and now have huge difficulties to overcome. Don't live in pity, wishing you were someone else. Start where you are, lean on God, and see what He will do in you.

The same God whose grace and power took Joseph to the top can also help you work your way past the worst spiritual obstacles. Call on Him for His forgiveness and help. With God on your side, you can overcome a bad start.

—*Mart DeHaan*

GAME PLAN

What are the two biggest roadblocks to spiritual success in your life? What would be the best approach to overcoming them?

From the Playbook:
Read Genesis 37:12–28.

DISSOLVED DREAMS

"In all things God works for the good of those who love him."
ROMANS 8:28

My Olympic dream was formed when I was a young girl playing basketball at a small village school in rural Alberta. For the next fourteen years the desire to one day become an Olympic athlete set the course of my life. My focus never wavered in times of struggle or failure. Rather, my resolve grew stronger, giving purpose to every challenge I faced along the way.

In the summer of 2003, as a member of the Canadian National Basketball Team, I came within two games of seeing my dream become reality at a qualifying tournament in Mexico. We needed a first-place finish to qualify. Instead, we lost by six points to Brazil in the semifinal. To make matters worse, although I had been a key player through-out the tournament, a change in strategy for the Brazil game left me on the side-line. Six points. Three baskets were all we needed. My heart broke as I was forced to helplessly watch my lifelong dream dissolve before me.

Filtering through the frustration, confusion, and crushing discouragement, I clearly sensed God reassuring me that He was still in control. Our view of any situation is so limited, and yet we let our hopes rise and fall on the whim of circumstances. From God's perspective, He sees the big picture—the beginning and the end all at once—and He works in all things "for the good of those who love him." I have to trust that, even as I live with my dissolved dreams.

—*Leighann Reimer, former pro basketball player*

> **GAME PLAN**
>
> Consider a time before you were a Christian when you were disappointed. How did you handle it? Since becoming a Christian, has your response to disappointment changed? What can you do to help yourself see the "big picture" in the middle of a disappointing situation?

From the Playbook:
Read Romans 8.

KIDS AND SPORTS

*"Whatever you do, work at it with all your heart,
as working for the Lord."* COLOSSIANS 3:23

In my twenty-six years of playing on the Ladies Professional Golfers Association (LPGA) Tour, I've seen many things that I like, but I've also observed things that bother me.

One thing that upsets me is the way some parents push their children to play golf. Too often, there is an over-emphasis on winning at an early age. It's as if a child is encouraged to start a pro career at age ten. Kids ought to be having fun playing golf at that age. It's not that youngsters shouldn't be encouraged to get better, it's just that winning shouldn't get blown out of proportion.

I've been taught to give my best with the talent God has given me—to be obedient to Him day-by-day. I think that's what we should be teaching our young people—not that they have to be a pro someday to be successful.

Kids are taught that if they want anything bad enough, they can have it. I don't believe that. Many other factors are involved. For example, you have to have some measure of talent. And you have to have the right temperament.

I don't think God wants us to think that way either. He wants us to give 100 percent, but that's it! We don't have to get all caught up in being "No. 1."

If we're highly talented and become No. 1, fine. But if we give our best and we're No. 100, that's fine too.

As long as we do our best for God's glory, we will be pleasing God and honoring Him—which is what we're supposed to be doing anyway.

—*Betsy King, LPGA Hall of Fame*

GAME PLAN

Do you know any youth sports athletes? How can you encourage them without pressuring them into thinking that they have to be the next Kobe Bryant or Betsy King or Cobi Jones?

From the Playbook:
Read Colossians 3.

HOW TO BE A PEACEMAKER

"Blessed are the peacemakers, for they will be called sons of God." MATTHEW 5:9

I had the privilege of competing against one of the greatest female athletes of all time. Her name is Jackie Joyner-Kersee. Jackie was a phenomenal athlete. She competed in the heptathlon, which is a grueling two-day, seven-event competition. Jackie participated in four Olympics and was a five-time Olympic medalist.

Apart from her athletic abilities, what impressed me the most about this remarkable woman was her welcoming and encouraging attitude. Often I would compete against Jackie in a hurdle race, and she would always approach me as a friend first, then as a competitor. Now don't get me wrong. She was a fierce competitor who always pursued the attitude of winning. But her attitude toward the athletes was always friendly. This posture was unusual because many athletes prefer to look at competitors as an enemy in order to gain the necessary edge needed for victory.

In my opinion, Jackie demonstrated the elements of peacemaking. Many times I found myself seeking her out at competitions because the aroma of love was prevalent. Her attitude helped me to compete better and treat my competitors with the same respect.

Similarly, our attitude is to be pleasing to the Lord. Our energies should be focused on winning His approval. Our efforts and desires to be peacemakers often act as a sweet fragrance that others, even our enemies, are drawn toward—and then are drawn toward Him.

—*LaVonna Martin-Floreal, Olympic silver medalist, track*

GAME PLAN

Would your friends call you a peacemaker? What are some things you can do in the next couple of days to show yourself to have the attitude of a peacemaker, even in tense situations?

From the Playbook:
Read and contemplate the Beatitudes: Matthew 5:1–12.

BEARING THE NAME

"Since we live by the Spirit, let us keep in step with the Spirit."
GALATIANS 5:25

I can still remember the first day I put on that USA jersey. I was so proud. It was a dream come true; an amazing honor to travel around the world, playing volleyball, and representing my country.

Everywhere we went, we bore the USA name. Because we represented the most powerful country in the world, fans and opposing teams watched us and held us to high standards. For some, we might be the only Americans they would ever encounter. People watched us closely on and off the court.

In order to uphold this high standard, we had team rules that everyone followed. Good sportsmanship was showcased by being respectful to the opponents and the officials. We had a no-swearing policy, and it was always important to portray a disciplined, organized, and clean-cut image.

As Christians we hold similar responsibilities as being a part of a team. We bear the name of Christ. People hold us to high standards and watch us closely. Some may think Christianity is about obeying a bunch of rules, but it is so much more. To bear Christ's name is an amazing honor. He has given us the ultimate gift of eternal life. Because of His amazing grace, we should always strive to please Him and represent His name to the best of our abilities.

Wear the name of Christ with pride for the amazing gift He has given. You just never know who's watching.

—*Val Kemper, former member, US national volleyball team*

GAME PLAN

Think back over the past couple of days. Did you represent Jesus Christ well? If not, what can you do better tomorrow to make sure people see Jesus in you?

From the Playbook:
Read Galatians 5:16–6:10.

ONE LITTLE GIRL—ONE BIG GOD

"[God] is able to do exceeding abundantly above all that we ask or think." EPHESIANS 3:20 (KJV)

A mother's heart was crushed when the doctors reported that her little three-year-old daughter was not responding to treatment and would die. She had contracted spinal meningitis and didn't even know her mother.

No amount of comfort could stop the little girl's crying. She was in great pain and too young to understand why. Her mother knew the only thing to do was pray and trust God for her little girl's life.

She stayed by her daughter's bedside and prayed through the night. Her daughter's cry turned to a wimper and finally was silenced. The doctors returned the next morning expecting her to have died in the night. To their surprise, she was peacefully sleeping. They rediagnosed her and told the mother, "She seems to be doing a little better. She has a 50–50 chance of making it, but if she comes through this, she will be mentally retarded and physically, she will never do what the normal child does."

The mother looked at the doctors with a slight smile across her face and nodded, "Uh-huh!" She knew that if God had brought her daughter out of death through the night, He had so much more for her in life.

This little girl grew up to become a world champion in track and win the gold and silver medals at the Olympic Games. She gave her life to Jesus at the age of six years old and today travels the world to minister to diversified people and world-class athletes. I know this because that little girl was me.

The promise of God is given to all believers. He will give you much more than you can ask or think because He wants His glory to be revealed in the lives of His children. Oh, how He loves you and me.

—*Madeline Mims, Olympic medalist, track*

GAME PLAN

"Father, I am Yours to do with as You will. Your will over my life be done, not mine. May my life glorify You in all that I do, say, and am. In Jesus' name. Amen."

From the Playbook:

Read: Philippians 3:7–14; Malachi 3:10; Luke 6:38.

THE SUCCESS OF DESIRE

"[Don't] grow weary and lose heart." HEBREWS 12:3

I'm inspired every time I recall the story of a remarkable female athlete named Wendy Stoker. In high school, she diligently practiced for four years to improve her skills as a diver. As a senior, she placed third in the Iowa girls state diving championship.

Wendy went on to attend the University of Florida, where she continued her hard work. While carrying a full load of classes, she earned the No. 2 position on the varsity diving squad. Her hard work was recognized in 2002 when she was inducted into the Iowa High School Swim Coaches Association Hall of Fame.

Perhaps the most amazing thing about Wendy Stoker, however, was her typing skills. She pounded out 45 words a minute on her typewriter—with her toes.

You see, Wendy Stoker was born without arms. Wendy's physical limitations could have held her back, but they didn't. Why? Because she possessed a main component to success—desire. Absolutely nothing of human greatness is achieved without it. With desire, we can succeed despite overwhelming limitations. Without it, we limit ourselves even though we may possess great capabilities.

Although most of us will never know the challenges Wendy Stoker faces each day, we all have our limitations, real or perceived. Our limitations can tempt us to give up desire. But when we lose desire we lose heart. That is one reason why the Bible encourages us to fix our eyes on Jesus so that we don't "grow weary and lose heart" (Hebrews 12:2–3).

Desire is the secret to success. Knowing Jesus is the secret to desire.

—*Jeff Olson*

GAME PLAN

Identify where you are tempted to give up desire because your limitations seem too great. Ask God for help in pressing forward.

From the Playbook:
Read Galatians 6:9.

WHO'S ON THE PEDESTAL?

"Do nothing out of selfish ambition or vain conceit, but in humility consider others better than yourselves." PHILIPPIANS 2:3

As an athlete, I find Philippians 2:3 to be an extremely challenging verse.

It seems to dictate the opposite of what I tend to believe about myself, especially going into competition. In fact, when an athlete considers her opponent to be better than herself, there is much sports psychology literature that states she has already lost before she has begun. A closer look at this verse, though, can help us see the heart of its message.

Webster defines *humility* as "respectful deference," that is, "courteous respect for another's opinion or judgment." I have always respected my opponents, so that's not a problem.

Considering them to be better than myself, however, is where my difficulty lies. Another verse helps us here. We are told in 1 Corinthians 1:31, "Let him who boasts boast in the Lord." There's my problem! Typically, I am far from boasting in the Lord. Considering others better than myself moves me off the pedestal I tend to put myself on and helps me realize I am the person God created me to be, nothing more and nothing less.

Whether in competition or otherwise, learn how to humbly consider others better than yourself. Do not degrade yourself or compromise your personal beliefs, but merely develop a respect for those against whom you compete or hold differing views. And always remember that your gifts—even your athletic skills—come from God, not yourself.

—*Jean Driscoll, eight-time Boston Marathon wheelchair champion*

GAME PLAN

Why should you consider others better than yourself? What does it mean to "boast in the Lord"?

From the Playbook:
Read Philippians 2:1–11.

THE TOP 10 LIST

"Love the Lord your God with all your heart and with all your soul and with all your mind." MATTHEW 22:37

USA Today recently compiled a list of the ten hardest things to do in sports.

10. Skiing in the downhill
9. Saving a penalty kick in soccer
8. Riding a bicycle in the Tour de France
7. Running in a marathon
6. Figure skating's quad spin toe loop
5. A return of serve in tennis
4. Hitting a long straight tee shot in golf
3. Pole vaulting
2. Driving a race car
1. Hitting a baseball at 95 mph

GAME PLAN

Maybe you've given in to temptation recently and you feel really discouraged and down about it. Tell God you're sorry and continue with the training program. Sinning doesn't mean you stay away from the Bible. Sinning means you read even more of the Bible to help you win against sin the next time.

God has a Top 10 list too. The ten laws or commandments are really the most basic things a person should do just to be a decent human being. Don't kill, steal, or lie are just a few. But we fail to master the ten rules. God's guidelines are too tough, too hard. Like trying to hit a major league fastball. We strike out. In Matthew 22:37–40 Jesus summed up the ten rules into two important ones. First, love God with all your heart, soul, and mind. Second, love your neighbor as yourself. Still, those are pretty hard to do.

Second Timothy 3:16 says that the Bible can teach, correct, and train you to be the person God wants you to be. In sports or life, there are some things that will be too hard for you to do. But what God wants you to do comes with a training program guaranteed to work. It's in the Bible.

—Dan Deal

From the Playbook:
Read Matthew 22:34–40; 2 Timothy 3:10–17.

DISCOVERING LIFE AFTER DEATH

"By prayer and petition, with thanksgiving, present your requests to God. And the peace of God, which transcends all understanding, will guard your hearts and your minds in Christ Jesus." PHILIPPIANS 4:6–7

There is such a thing as life after death. When a loved one dies, we might feel that our own life has been taken away from us. But the peace of God will restore the goodness of our life to us.

I had to travel through a time when I had to face and conquer the doubts that my mom's death brought into my life. Once I realized that this is possible only through Christ, I began to live again.

I was devastated by the death of my mom in 1996. Never once had she been sick. I lost my mom to what doctors call Legionnaire's disease (double pneumonia). I was saddened, I was angry, I was bitter, and I was mad at God. I turned away from Him and refused to acknowledge that spiritually I was dying. I shut the Holy Bible with no intentions of opening it anytime soon.

There were moments when I could not breathe when I thought about her not being a part of my life. I would almost feel as if I was having a nervous breakdown. As time passed, I realized that I was only sinking further into despair—so I began to turn to my only hope. As I began to pray and seek God's face, I found myself being more able to handle the fact that my mother was gone.

God began to instill a peace inside of me. That kind of peace "surpasses all understanding, [and] will guard your hearts and minds through Christ Jesus" (Philippians 4:7 NKJV).

We must rely on God to see us through life's difficult situations.

When I did that, I began to live again and see that there was life for me after my mom's death.

—*Charlotte Smith, former WNBA forward*

GAME PLAN

What is seeming to take the joy out of your life? How can I let Philippians 4:7 help me with that? Have you experienced grief recently? Is it possible to gain God's peace?

From the Playbook:
Read Psalm 23 if you need any comfort that relates to death.

THROWING IN THE KNEEPADS?

"Run in such a way as to get the prize." 1 CORINTHIANS 9:24

It had been a long trip. Ten days in Switzerland with eight volleyball matches down and one to go.

After playing eleven years of competitive sports, for the first time ever I was "riding the pine." Not only did I sit the bench, I was the only player who had not played the entire trip. My confidence level was at an all-time low. I was ready to throw in the kneepads, put volleyball behind me, and forget my Olympic dreams.

The night before our final match was a night I'll never forget. I sat out on the terrace of our hotel overlooking Lake Geneva and surrounded by the Swiss Alps. In the midst of God's amazing creation I felt His presence. I opened my Bible and cried out to Him through all of my hurt and frustration. He spoke to me strongly through His Word: "Do you not know that in a race all the runners run, but only one gets the prize? Run in such a way as to get the prize" (1 Corinthians 9:24).

I began to realize that I was in the same race as my teammates. We were all running together. We all wanted to play. We all wanted to win. However, which of us played was up to the coach. Was I about to quit over one disappointing tournament? No! Through God's inspiring Word, my attitude did a 180-degree turn that night in Switzerland. I began to accept my role, and I continued to press on.

It's amazing how similar our spiritual journey is to the ups and downs in athletics. In sports and in life, when we face hardship and trials, it is tempting to quit. We must be encouraged to change our attitude. We must trust that God will strengthen us as we continue to run for our eternal prize. We must not quit.

—*Val Kemper, former member, US national volleyball team*

GAME PLAN

Are you ready to quit something important because you are discouraged? Have you spoken with God about this and asked Him to give you strength? Can you see how God's name can be glorified if you stick with it?

From the Playbook:
Read 1 Corinthians 9:19–27.

TELL YOUR FRIENDS!

"[Jesus] said unto them, 'Go into all the world and preach the good news to all creation.'" MARK 16:15

*J*esus commands Christians to "go into all the world and preach the good news to all creation. Whoever believes and is baptized will be saved, but whoever does not believe will be condemned" (Mark 16:15–16).

Before the 2000 Olympics began, I knew that if I made the team I was going to give all the glory to my Lord and Savior Jesus Christ. I had the opportunity to play in front of the world in the gold medal game in Sydney and relied on God's strength to play and be a witness for Him.

Since bringing home Olympic gold medals with the USA Softball Team, all of us on the team have had many opportunities for speaking engagements and media events. Some of my teammates have endorsements with shoe companies, most of us have contracts with bat companies like Worth Inc., we have had some appearances on TV, and we have been featured in magazines.

But let me tell you about a special opportunity. A couple weeks after I was home, I had the opportunity to speak at the church my husband Tommy and I attend, Harvest Christian Fellowship in Riverside, California. As I stood up in front of a couple thousand people and started to share what God has done in my life and about my Olympic experience, I knew that this was the greatest opportunity I could have.

The media appearances are great for a short time, but it's God's message of eternal life that truly matters. Sharing that message is something we can all do.

Struggling with wondering how to spread the good news? Just tell the people in your world about Jesus. That's all you're expected to do.

—*Leah O'Brien-Amico, Olympic gold medalist, softball*

GAME PLAN

Is there someone who needs to hear the gospel from you via conversation, e-mail, letter, or phone call? Why not give yourself a deadline to spread the good news with that person?

From the Playbook:
Read Acts 8:26–40.

STRONG AND COURAGEOUS

"Be strong and very courageous." JOSHUA 1:7

I remember it like it was yesterday. Sunday, September 22, 2002. Final round of the Solheim Cup.

Individual singles matches were all that were left to decide the team winner. I drew Annika Sorenstam, the world's No. 1 female golfer. The media and world thought this was the biggest mismatch of the day. But not for me or my US teammates. Though my support seemed small, it was plentiful. I knew God would never give me anything He and I could not face together.

So with confidence, I entered the match the underdog and played with the strength and fire only the Holy Spirit could ignite. My husband, Nate (who was also my caddie), my captain, my team, my family, and friends all offered me the support and encouragement I would need to face this challenge.

I remember going to sleep the night before this final match and being inspired by the great story of David and Goliath (1 Samuel 17). David, like me, was certainly the underdog taking on the big, mighty giant Goliath. Outsized and destined to be defeated, David stood strong and with the hand of God on his side, successfully defeated Goliath.

Now, David did not have the support of his teammates as I did, but he did prevail—thanks to his faith and trust in God. I was fortunate to have the support of my teammates, plus the power of God working through me to match Annika shot for shot. We went on to halve the match, which was like a victory for me—and eventually it helped lead to the win for the US team.

The essence of my story is standing strong in the face of challenges and battles. With God's help, you can be victorious in every thing you do, even when the deck is stacked against you. Be strong and courageous! (Joshua 1:7).

—*Wendy Ward, LPGA golfer*

GAME PLAN

What is your huge opposition today? A meeting with the boss? A job interview? A huge test? A big game? An illness? We all face Goliaths in life. The question is whether we go up against our problems alone or with God next to us.

From the Playbook:
Read 1 Samuel 17.

BATTLING BACK FROM THE BRINK

"We rejoice in our sufferings, because we know that suffering produces perseverance." ROMANS 5:3

My softball teammates and I felt confident as we headed into the 2000 Olympics in Sydney, Australia. As reigning Olympic Champions and World Champions, we knew what it took to win.

We never would have believed that halfway through the Games we would be on the brink of elimination.

After winning 112 games in a row, including the first two games in Sydney, we lost three straight games. One more loss and our team would be eliminated before the medal round.

After our third loss, a teammate read to the team out loud on the bus Romans 5:3-4, which says, "We also rejoice in our sufferings because we know that suffering produces perseverance; perseverance, character; and character, hope." We needed to persevere, and we needed hope.

We did persevere. We went on to beat Japan in the championship game, and we received the gold medals after the game.

In life you can receive a prize much greater than an Olympic gold medal, the prize of eternal life. After persevering through life's trials, you, like the apostle Paul, will be able to declare, "I have fought the good fight, I have finished the race, I have kept the faith. Now there is in store for me the crown of righteousness, which the Lord, the righteous Judge, will award to me on that day" (2 Timothy 4:7-8).

Despite the setbacks you might face today, keep trusting the Lord. He has a fantastic reward waiting for you in heaven.

—*Leah O'Brien-Amico, Olympic gold medalist, softball*

GAME PLAN

What is your biggest struggle this week? Does it sometimes make you want to stop trusting God? Remember, that would be the worst thing you could ever do. Hold on.

From the Playbook:

Read James 1:2-18.

GODLY INSPIRATION

"Follow my example, as I follow the example of Christ."
1 CORINTHIANS 11:1

All coaches, whether they embrace the responsibility or not, play a role in directing and shaping the athletes they work with. Coaches either build up or tear players down. They empower or weaken others by their words and the example they set. They create an environment that inspires a person to excel or fail. Coaches demonstrate how to handle success and how to deal with losses; in short, they set the tone for the team.

Great coaches tap hidden potential and get the best investments on obvious talent. They give their athletes a vision of something larger than themselves and define a mission worth pursuing. They turn doubters into believers. Great coaches are strong leaders and inspire great results.

NFL punter Josh Bidwell says, "Without a question, my high school coach had the biggest influence on my life from a football perspective. He knew the game and brought out the best in the players. But the biggest factor for me was that he was a strong man of God with a tremendous amount of integrity that I admired. He never compromised his faith—that was first and foremost in his life. I think that spoke louder than anything. He was available to meet with me one-on-one to talk about my growth as a player, a Christian, and a person."

In 1 Corinthians 11:1 Paul says, "Follow my example as I follow the example of Christ." Josh Bidwell found an example in his coach of a man who follows Christ. Who in your life models a consistent Christian walk? What can you learn from that person?

—*Roxanne Robbins*

GAME PLAN

Write a letter to a person who has influenced you to walk more closely with God because of their example. Thank them and give specific ways they have helped you mature in your own faith.

From the Playbook:
Read Titus 2.

WHEN I AM AFRAID

"The Lord is my helper; I will not be afraid." HEBREWS **13:6**

aura Wilkinson surprised everyone in Sydney, Australia, at the 2000 Olympic Games. She entered the finals of the platform diving competition of the Games in fifth place. There seemed to be no way Laura could reach the top of the field.

But as Wilkinson watched her competitors begin making major errors with their dives, she began to believe there was still a chance for her to win.

"I decided not to pay attention to the scoreboard," she says. "I was going to just put together my best list and do the best I could."

That was just the strategy Laura needed. She strung together five solid dives, and she won the gold medal.

What proved to be the greatest surprise of the night was still to come. While being interviewed following her final dive for Olympic glory, Laura was asked what she was thinking as she stood on the platform. She responded, "I can do all things through Christ who strengthens me" (Philippians 4:13 NKJV).

Wilkinson saw the power of God carry her through a time when she needed strength. "There are several Bible verses I keep close to me," she says. "When I get nervous or scared, I think of Isaiah 41:10. God promises to always be with me when I'm afraid. That means the impossible is possible," she says. "During the Olympics it was especially true."

We're not talking magic words here. We're talking about asking the God of the universe to work, through the Holy Spirit, in our lives. There is nothing that we cannot get through when we allow God's awesome presence to accompany us.

—*Dave Branon*

GAME PLAN

What do you fear the most? How often do you step back and pray, asking for God to calm your heart when that fear strikes?

From the Playbook:
Read Psalm 46.

GOD HAS A PLAN FOR YOU

"All the days ordained for me were written in your book before one of them came to be." PSALM 139:16

"or I know the plans I have for you,' declares the Lord, 'plans to prosper you and not to harm you, plans to give you a hope and a future'" (Jeremiah 29:11). Those words have taken on special meaning for me because they remind me how much God cares.

At the 2000 Olympic Games in Sydney, Australia, we had a very special batgirl for our game against Cuba. Katie, a sixteen-year-old from Texas, and her family were flown out to Australia to watch us play.

Although she looked completely healthy and wore a smile on her face, Katie had undergone the battle of her life. She had fought cancer, and when she was in Australia, Katie was in remission. She was involved in the Make-a-Wish Foundation, which had granted her wish to meet the United States Olympic softball team.

Before the game against Cuba, I asked her if she wanted to join our team in our pregame prayer, and she accepted. As I knelt down and prayed to the Lord, I was humbled by the peace of this young girl. The biggest worry for myself was winning a softball game, and this girl was and is fighting for her life.

Her strength, along with an important verse in God's Word, has taught me much about life. I can rejoice daily because I know that "all of the days ordained for me were written in [His] book before one of them came to be" (Psalm 139:16).

God has a plan for each person. I am thankful that I can trust each day to Him—both on earth and in eternity.

—*Leah O'Brien-Amico, Olympic gold medalist, softball*

GAME PLAN

What troubles you about today? Pray this prayer: "Lord, thank You for today. I know You've given it to me for a reason. Help me to enjoy it as a special gift from You. And help me to live for You today."

From the Playbook:
Read Psalm 139.

WATCH YOUR MOUTH

"The Lord said to [Moses], 'Who gave man his mouth?'"
EXODUS 4:11

It is commonplace these days to be watching a televised sporting event in which the cameras zoom in on two athletes "trash talking" one another. Often the exchange is examined in a replay so the announcers can get a sense of how it started. Words can certainly draw attention to the individuals involved in the verbal skirmish.

There are many verses in the Bible that address the significance of the words we speak. For example, Ephesians 4:29 says, "Do not let any unwholesome talk come out of your mouths, but only what is helpful for building others up according to their needs, that it may benefit those who listen." Clearly, Paul's words tell us that God cares what we say and how our words affect those around us.

Isn't it interesting, though, as James pointed out, that "out of the same mouth come praise and cursing"? (James 3:10). We praise God and curse men (or vice versa) with the same mouth. What an irony!

GAME PLAN

Can you think of a time when you lost control of your words? What kind of damage did you cause? Why are the words you speak important to God?

During the course of our lives, there will inevitably be situations that test our self-control, especially in the midst of heated sports competition. Sometimes, we lose control of our thoughts and then our mouths when we are tired, off-guard, and vulnerable.

That's why we must train ourselves now—in the cool sensibility of a calm moment far from the heat of battle—to be pure in speech and deed. People are watching, and your example could either be cause for praising or cursing. It could lead them to or away from the Savior.

That's why we must watch what we say.
—*Jean Driscoll, eight-time Boston Marathon wheelchair champion*

From the Playbook:
Read James 3:4–11.

BUCHAREST PERSPECTIVE

"Has not God chosen those who are poor in the eyes of the world to be rich in faith?" JAMES 2:5

Hall of Fame golfer Betsy King has given of herself for the past few years traveling to Europe—especially to Romania—to help children and provide spiritual assistance. She tells about one such experience.

Eight other players on the LPGA Tour and I first went to Romania not knowing exactly what we would be doing. We were with a group that had been involved in adoptions of children in the United States.

The first time we went, we stayed with families and visited orphanages. We got to meet quite a few children, and we played with the kids and supplied some support to the ministry that was working there.

The second time we went, we again went to some orphanages and to a hospital. We sang for the children, which wasn't our forte. We sang for youth groups and at a formal church service in Bucharest.

The thing that stands out as we take these trips is the word *perspective*. We have to put things into perspective in terms of what's really important in life.

The first year, I went to Romania after winning a tournament in Japan, and within 48 hours I was on the streets of Bucharest, meeting street kids—kids as young as five years old who had no place to live. God used that to show me that winning a golf tournament isn't all that important.

We sang the song, "Give Thanks," and one of the lines is "let the poor say I am rich," and for them, it is so true. They're so financially poor, yet they're rich in their faith and commitment to the Lord.

Now, that's a great perspective!

—*Betsy King, LPGA Hall of Fame*

GAME PLAN

Have you thought about being involved in some kind of missions trip? Why not plan to see if you can put that in your schedule for next year.

From the Playbook:
Read James 2:1–13.

FREE OR BOUND?

"He has sent me to bind up the brokenhearted." Isaiah 61:1

Have you ever experienced a broken heart? I love how the Lord lets us know that He not only came to save the lost but also to heal the brokenhearted! (See Psalm 34:18.) He cares about our wounds and wants to bring us healing.

Many of us have wounds that we cover with the bandage of sports. We work out like crazy, we drive ourselves beyond where others would stop, and we carry anger inside and it manifests as aggression.

Oh, I've been there. For years the game was the thing that saved me from going over the edge. We all find something to deal with our hurts. I used softball and baseball. But the problem is, it is all temporary. We continue to reapply a new bandage because the wound just seems to keep splitting open. The healing never takes place.

But Jesus has come to heal our hearts. When we allow him to apply His medicine, we find healing. There will forever remain a scar, but that scar tells a story, a testimony of the healing power of Jesus.

So if you struggle with sin that afflicts you from the outside or sin you've committed, allow Jesus and His truth to bring healing to your bones. Galatians 5:1 says, "It is for freedom that Christ has set us free. Stand firm, then, and do not let yourselves be burdened again by a yoke of slavery." When we allow God to free us up, we live and play with more joy and have more peace.

Are you bound by sin or free in Christ?

—*Kim Braatz-Voisard, former pro baseball player*

> **GAME PLAN**
>
> Does something seem to have its grip on you? Have you asked Jesus to free you from its clutches—and then depended on His Holy Spirit to give you the strength to remain free?

From the Playbook:
Read 2 Corinthians 3:7–18.

FROM BAD TO GOOD

"In all things God works for the good of those who love him."
ROMANS 8:28

GAME PLAN

What is happening in your life this week that looks bad but that God can turn into good? It takes real faith and trust to see that happen. Are you willing to try?

At the end of my first year of racing, I was invited to a triathlon in Japan—all expenses paid. I was the only US female representative, so it was quite an honor. There was one catch: The race was almost three times as long as any race I had ever done. It would be a challenge just to finish, but I was game!

When I arrived in Japan, I decided to loosen up in the hotel pool. On my last flipturn, as my feet came over I whacked my heel down hard on the edge. I had never in twelve years of swimming hit my heel. It hurt just to walk on it, let alone run sixteen miles at the end of the triathlon.

At first I cried out to God and asked why this happened. In reading the Bible that night, I discovered today's verse. "In all things"—including racing a triathlon with a hurt heal—"God works for the good of those who love him." All I could do was put my faith in God that He would turn this situation around to His good, because I loved Him and trusted Him.

On race day I swam and biked well, but the real test was the run. When I put on my shoes, I felt no pain. Skeptics might say it was adrenaline, but I ran for sixteen pain-free miles—four miles longer than my longest run ever. Adrenaline can't do that, but the Lord can.

The Lord created a situation that I thought was bad. He did it so my faith and trust in Him could be strengthened. That's for my good. But He also gave me a story of triumph (well, second place in this case), to encourage others that "in all things God works for the good of those who love him."

—*Barb Lindquist, Olympic triathlete*

From the Playbook:
Read Romans 8:28–39.

RUN THE RIGHT PLAY

"Among you there must not be even a hint of sexual immorality." EPHESIANS 5:3

A few years ago, a study of prime-time TV shows (7:00 to 10:00 PM) revealed that approximately 2,000 TV episodes illustrated sexual behavior. Of these episodes, 80 percent of them depicted people who were unmarried.

Let's talk about one popular show during that time: *Coach*. The coach was living with his girlfriend—and their sexual relationship was assumed and accepted. The message was clear: You have permission to engage in sex outside of marriage.

God does not give this permission. In the Bible, the message is clear: Don't run that play (sexual intimacy) until you are married. Scripture is plain on this matter—sex is designed for a man and a woman within the confines of marriage (Genesis 2:24). Within marriage God's Word says in essence: Run that play. Run it often (read Hebrews 13:4).

Sex is a beautiful gift designed by God. It has always been a big deal to Him. He created it for basically three reasons:

1. Procreation. Precious children created in God's own image with an eternal soul (Genesis 9:1).

2. Marital pleasure. That special bond of security and intimacy reserved for a husband and wife (Song of Songs).

3. Symbolizing the union of Christ. The Bridegroom becoming one with His bride: the church (Ephesians 5:25).

Every time we think or act on a sexual impulse, we ought to be reminded of our spiritual intimacy with Jesus Christ.

Run the only play that results in true sexual intimacy—within marriage.
—*Ron Brown, assistant college football coach*

> **GAME PLAN**
>
> **Where are you getting your information about what is acceptable sexual behavior? From TV? The movies? Songs? Or from the Word of God?**

From the Playbook:
Read 1 Corinthians 7:12–20.

ONLY AS A RESULT OF FAITH

"Faith is being sure of what we hope for." HEBREWS 11:1

*J*ean Driscoll was born with spina bifida. Doctors predicted she would never walk and that she would most likely remain dependent on her parents her entire life.

Despite the odds, Jean became one of the world's most decorated athletes. She won the wheelchair division of the prestigious Boston Marathon eight times and medaled in three Olympic games. Jean says her success in racing was built on the foundation of her faith and a passage of Scripture that has become her personal creed: "Faith is being sure of what we hope for and certain of what we do not see" (Hebrews 11:1). "That verse helped me see my disability through different lenses," Jean says. "Walking is overrated. Jesus Christ suffered and died on the cross for my sin. I now know, by faith, that He lives in me and gives me grace day by day."

For most of Jean's life, people placed limitations on her. "I went from feeling worthless to having Olympic medals and a fan base. It blows me away that people recognize me when I go to the grocery store." With her success has come responsibility. Jean welcomes the opportunity to be a role model who shows how to live up to the motto she includes with her autograph: "Dream Big and Work Hard."

"For young people and adults," Jean says, "the biggest limitations are the ones you place on yourself. You have to experience failure before you can appreciate success."

Like Jean did, take time to reflect on a trial or failure that helped you appreciate the success God has given you.

—*Roxanne Robbins*

GAME PLAN

Take a step of faith this week. Do something you know you should do but have been afraid to do. Afterward, write down what God taught you about faith through this exercise.

From the Playbook:
See who made the "Hall of Faith" in Hebrews 11.

TRUSTING GOD'S PLAN

"Trust in the Lord with all your heart." PROVERBS 3:5

Trust is a difficult concept to grasp. It is even harder when the chips are down.

I remember the second time I made it through Qualifying School for the LPGA Tour. I had shot 83 the first day, and the prospects of keeping my card on Tour weren't looking very bright. After much prayer and reflection, I decided that there wasn't much I could control, and I decided that I would give the rest of the week over to God.

The only thing I could control was to discipline myself to stay committed and play every shot to the best of my ability. How the rest of the field did was something that I could not control. I knew that God held my future in His hands and that no matter what happened, He knew what was best for me. After deciding that I would yield control to God, a tremendous burden was lifted from me because I knew that I no longer had to worry. All I had to do was my very best and trust that God knew the best plan and way for me.

The next day I shot a 67, and I picked up my first career hole-in-one. I also played well the remaining two days, and I was able to keep my card for the following season.

There is something freeing about letting go and letting God handle your concerns. It is hard to do, because we all want to exercise some form of control in our lives. If we could just learn to let God be in charge, we would have less to worry about in our lives. After all, He's our Maker. Of course He knows the best plan for our lives.

—*Siew-Ai Lim, former LPGA golfer*

GAME PLAN

What area of your life are you having trouble giving up to God? Is it a matter of trust or a matter of simply not wanting to let go?

From the Playbook:
Read Proverbs 16:1–9.

THE GIRLS HAVE GAME

"Don't show favoritism." JAMES 2:1

My daughter's first basketball game of the season was going to be brutal to watch.

At least that's what I thought. In my mind I saw a mix of soccer and rugby being played on a basketball court. This brand of basketball was hardly ready for a debut on the X-Games. More like the Z-Games. Zzzzzzzzzz. Wake me up when it's over.

But to my utter amazement I saw bounce passes, picks being set, and even a made 3-pointer. The girls do have game. The problem was my prejudice. I didn't even realize it at first.

I think a lot of us are that way. I'm all for my daughter playing sports. Girls have talent, no question about it. But I had pre-judged this group of eighth-grade girls. Yeah, I was bad and I admit it. Sometimes I'm not too smart.

This whole thing got me thinking deeper. About me, about us as humans, and about those of us who say we're Christians. Are we willing to admit the prejudice that may be in our spiritual lives?

In his book *Growing Slowly Wise,* author David Roper expounds on the subject of pre-judging. He says, "Prejudice, whether elitism, sexism, ageism, or racism, is not a minor fault. It's serious sin. To justify and defend it, rather than repent of it suggests that I may not be a Christian at all. James minces no words. I can't be a bigot and call myself a believer."

I told my daughter I was sorry for thinking all I'd see at her game was a rugby scrum on a basketball court.

—Dan Deal

GAME PLAN

Jesus tells each of us to act and speak in mercy. The reason is, we're judged by the same standard that we use to pre-judge others.

From the Playbook:
Read James 2:1–13 and Matthew 5:7.

THEY CALL ME COACH

"Your word is a lamp to my feet." PSALM 119:105

There they were, 12 girls waiting for the coach (me!) to start our first soccer practice. I was expecting a great year; we had some talented young ladies on the team.

So, filled with hope, I blew my whistle. There was that one little problem though. I'd never played organized soccer . . . ever! But I had an ace up my sleeve. These girls didn't need much coaching, I thought. They've all played for years, I figured. It would be simple. Or so I hoped.

I had only one drill to work on at our first practice. It took about 20 minutes. That left 1 hour and 40 minutes to kill. So I handed out jerseys. We drank some water. I handed out the schedule. We got another drink. It got so bad that half the girls sat down on the field and started talking about which boys they liked at school. Then one girl quit the team. Where was that ace again?

I had to take action. I went to the library and checked out a book on soccer. As I read, I learned some of the basic rules, simple strategies, and most important for me, coaching drills. I needed the book.

A couple of months later, I saw a parallel between my coaching experience and my life. I think it applies to each of our lives. We need help to live this life or it soon spirals out of control. There's a Book that will give you everything you need. It's called the Bible. As you read the Bible, you'll find a strategy for life that really works. We all need the Book.

—*Dan Deal*

GAME PLAN

Find your Bible and turn to the book of Proverbs. Start reading, and when you see a good coaching tip, write it down. You can begin your own personal playbook from the Bible.

From the Playbook:
Read 2 Timothy 3:16–17.

A THANKS REMINDER

"I have learned the secret of being content in any and every situation." PHILIPPIANS 4:12

During a recent basketball game, I observed the variety of fans gathering in the stands. One man in particular caught my eye; his crumpled hands, shriveled and weakened body made him quite unlike those around him. I watched him weave his way closer to the court, awkwardly steering his wheelchair as he maneuvered a joystick with his chin.

I was struck by this image. Here was a man who, without an obvious miracle, would never leave the chair he was sitting in, and here I was running freely without pain, enjoying an activity that I quite often take for granted.

I was humbled by the thought. How many times have I complained about running too many lines or having sore muscles or even the inconvenience of traveling for a game? Despite this man's circumstances, he sat there with a smile on his face enjoying every moment of the game.

We have received from God blessings beyond our imagination, yet somehow we manage to find something to complain about. God has asked us to be content in all circumstances, whether in plenty or in want. Often I need to remind myself that God has placed me where He wants me, and I am to be thankful for all He has given me.

No matter what your lot is in life, take a moment to think about all the blessings in your life. Learn to rely on God; He knows what is best for each of us, and He promises to give us strength to joyfully live each day.

— *Leighann Reimer, former pro basketball player*

GAME PLAN

What blessings has God placed in your life today? How can you find true contentment where you are right at this moment? Have you taken the time to thank God for all He has given you?

From the Playbook:

For more on this topic see 1 Timothy 6:6, 8 and Hebrews 13:5.

THE POWER OF THE WORD

"The words I have spoken to you are spirit and they are life."
JOHN 6:63

Have you ever had a coach who hurt you with harsh words? Or did you have a coach who spoke carefully and lifted you up? It's been said that it takes ten positive phrases to knock out a negative one.

During my many years of coaching, I've come across a number of stories that demonstrate how powerful an encouraging word can be. Recently, I was told about a young girl who attended a basketball camp. She was participating in a one-minute shooting contest and was the least talented player on the court, but she put forth her best effort. After several attempts, she was close to beating her previous best score with time left on the clock. Her counselor shouted out, "You're dangerous!" She heard those words and proceeded to drain the last few buckets. Afterward, she reported her new best score to the head coach and said with a straight face, "Coach, I'm dangerous."

That's a humorous story, but it illustrates trust. That girl believed what her counselor told her. And we can believe Christ, who said, "The words I have spoken to you are spirit and they are life" (John 6:63).

We can trust that what God says in His Word is the truth for all. One day, the entire world will realize it. For now, let's speak words that build up those around us—strangers and friends alike. Mark my word, there will come a time when we will be very glad that we spoke words full of the Spirit and life.

—*Sue Semrau, women's college basketball coach*

GAME PLAN

Who needs you to speak up to them so you can share with them the power of God's Word?

From the Playbook:
Read Psalm 119:89–96.

RUN AND JUMP

"The wolf attacks the flock and scatters it." JOHN **10:12**

The basketball huddle: "Okay, here's the plan. Full-court pressure; run and jump. We're looking for the steal or the turnover. Force them to dribble. Push them beyond their limit of control. Remember—jump only when the dribbler is out of control or they have lost their downcourt vision! Don't let up; this game is ours."

The enemy's huddle: "Okay, here's the plan. Full-court pressure; run and jump. We're looking to steal, kill, and destroy. Force them to go it alone. Force them away from help. Push them beyond their limit to resist temptation. Remember—attack only when the opponents are already weakened or when they have lost sight of their purpose. Don't give up. We're not far behind; this game is ours!"

I find it interesting how much the sports tactics we talk about and watch are similar to the tactics of the spiritual realm.

Think about it. Can you identify with full-court pressure in your life? The Bible clearly explains that the enemy is real and "prowls around like a roaring lion looking for someone to devour" (1 Peter 5:8). Satan and his team are constantly conjuring up plans to lead the whole world astray (Revelation 12:9). If you are finding yourself rattled by Satan's pressure, remember to keep your head up, look for your teammates, and protect yourself with the heavenly armor (Ephesians 6:10–18).

"Thanks be to God! He gives us the victory through our Lord Jesus Christ" (1 Corinthians 15:57).

—*Molly Ramseyer*

GAME PLAN

In what specific area of your life do you feel Satan's pressure? When in that situation, memorize and recite James 4:7, "Resist the devil, and he will flee from you."

From the Playbook:

Read Ephesians 6:10–18 and put on each piece of armor before you leave your house this week!

130

THE GREATEST MOMENT IN HISTORY

"Let's . . . see this thing that has happened." LUKE 2:15

- US Hockey's "Miracle on Ice"
- Mary Lou Retton's "Vault Without Fault"
- Mark McGwire's record-breaking 62nd home run.

Those are some of the greatest moments in the history of sports. If you were fortunate enough to witness one of these phenomenal events, you know you'll never forget that thrilling moment. We still get chills when we see video of Mary Lou's remarkable vault or when we hear Al Michaels exalt, "Do you believe in miracles? Yes!"

But no matter how awesome the sports moment, no "miracle" can ever compare to the truly supernatural miracle we celebrate each December 25.

On that stupendous day 2,000 years ago, in a little town called Bethlehem, a few shepherds were given a first-hand announcement of the greatest moment in the history of the world—the birth of Jesus!

Since the Garden of Eden, God's people had been waiting for the Messiah. For thousands of years, the prophets had predicted it. Finally the moment had arrived: "When the time had finally come, God sent his Son . . ." (Galatians 4:4).

What a mind-boggling experience for these shepherds! To be among the first to see the baby Jesus, God in the flesh! He had come to set us free from the bondage of sin and death—to reconcile us to God. He brought hope and peace—and the promise of everlasting life. Now that's a moment to celebrate!

Do you believe in miracles? There's never been one like what happened on that first Christmas day.

—*Christin Ditchfield*

GAME PLAN

This Christmas, don't miss the reason for the season. Before opening your presents, take time to re-read the story of Jesus' birth in Luke 2. Then thank God for His "indescribable gift!"

From the Playbook:
Read Luke 2:1–20; Matthew 2:1–12.

WHAT GOD HATES

"There are six things the Lord hates." PROVERBS **6:16**

There are six things the Lord hates, seven that are detestable to him: haughty eyes, a lying tongue, hands that shed innocent blood, a heart that devises wicked schemes, feet that are quick to rush into evil, a false witness who pours out lies, and a man who stirs up dissension among brothers" (Proverbs 6:16–19).

What enters your mind as you read these words, knowing that God *hates* these behaviors? Do you find yourself thinking of times, perhaps even recently, when you did the very thing God abhors? It's convicting that the Lord puts "shedding innocent blood" and spreading "dissension among brothers" in the same list. One clearly seems more heinously wrong than the other. But let's focus on the seventh thing listed: spreading dissension among brothers. What does this mean? "Dissension," which is translated "strife" in some Bible versions, is defined as "a bitter, sometimes violent conflict. An act of contention. Exertion for superiority."

On a sports team, it could take the form of turning your teammates against another player so you'll end up on top. Even if the argument or hard feelings only exist between you and the other person, everyone on your team feels the tension, and that is strife. Consider how you're treating your teammates and the other people in your life. If you're creating strife, ask the Lord for wisdom to behave differently and act on the guidance He gives you.

—*Roxanne Robbins*

GAME PLAN

Reflect on a relationship that's been difficult for you. Ask God to bring healing and then write out steps you can take to make things better.

From the Playbook:
Read Proverbs 6:12–19.

WHY AM I HERE?

"Therefore go and make disciples." MATTHEW 28:19

Why am I here?"

I was asked this question once, and I answered the question rather hurriedly, yet correctly. My response was, "To make an impact on this world, to change lives. We were not put here just to exist or to gain personal satisfaction from the many things of this world. But we were put here to be an extension of Christ."

Before Jesus ascended into heaven shortly after His resurrection, He gave what we have come to call "The Great Commission." It says that we were put here to continue what Christ started while on earth—to be ministers of God's Word and to lead people to Christ throughout the world.

In 2001, the WNBA gave a T-shirt to all players that read, "The WNBA: This is who I am." As athletes, many of us believe this slogan. We spend countless hours preparing our body and mind to meet next season's athletic challenges, and that's okay.

But what about us as Christians? We fail to spend twenty minutes a day getting connected with Christ to make sure we are prepared to meet life's daily challenges. The sport world is so enticing that we forget that we are disciples first and athletes second. And we forget that our sport is not why God put us here, but it is the avenue He gave us to bring glory to Him through our play and our discipleship to others.

GAME PLAN

Why are you where you are? Do you know how God can use you where you are to glorify Him? What would have to change for that to happen?

If you are an athlete, begin to use the platform God has given you as your place of ministry. Be an extension of Christ and fulfill His Great Commission. It's the reason you are here.

—*Kedra Holland-Corn, former WNBA player*

From the Playbook:
Read Matthew 28:16–20.

WHAT IS YOUR LEGACY?

"For to me, to live is Christ and to die is gain."
PHILIPPIANS 1:21

A legacy might be defined in a dictionary as anything that is handed down from an ancestor. It could be described as what you are remembered for. Perhaps the best description that I have heard is that your legacy is the dash or hyphen that sits between your date of birth and the date of death on your tombstone.

What is it that you are living for? Is it for professional progress, personal glory, or personal possessions? Are you striving to be the best employee or the best athlete or the best "something else" that one day will mean nothing? What is life to you?

The apostle Paul stated his purpose in Philippians 1:21 when he said, "For to me, to live is Christ and to die is gain." I believe it was Paul's desire and sole aim in life to glorify Jesus Christ in all that he did. Paul made it his purpose to imitate Christ and to emulate the humility, love, and compassion of Jesus. Paul desired and purposed to spread the gospel of Jesus Christ. He wanted others to know of God's love and gift of grace.

Paul had committed to make Jesus Christ his life. To him, Christ was life. What a legacy!
—*Bill Sampen, former major league pitcher*

GAME PLAN

Which of the two verses from the Playbook best describes you, Philippians 1:21, or Philippians 2:21? One of these verses most accurately describes our life and the legacy that we are preparing to leave. Are you comfortable with the legacy you are preparing to hand down? Are you willing to change it?

From the Playbook:

Read Philippians 1.
Compare Philippians 1:21, "For to me, to live is Christ"
to Philippians 2:21, "For everyone looks out for his
own interests, not those of Jesus Christ."

LOOKING AHEAD

"I press on toward the goal to win the prize."
PHILIPPIANS 3:13–14

When I reflect on my twenty-year career as a track and field athlete, what sticks with me the most is facing the challenging transition of moving from competitive life to regular life.

I have struggled with being a "normal" person. Many of these struggles include the normalcy of everyday living. My role as a wife, mother, and full-time working woman—combined with the lack of notoriety, international travel, and the thrill of competition—has presented many challenges. Sometimes it has even created fear in me.

But there is one future transition coming—one that I am certain will contain no fear. I am speaking of my transition someday into the presence of my heavenly Father. Although I am challenged by this life, I look forward to seeing my Savior face to face. Although the desire for death is not imminent for me, I am secure in knowing that the current challenges I face will cease to exist on the day I enter heaven. The longing and voids I sometimes feel because of no longer being an elite level athlete will be transformed into joy.

I rejoice in knowing that I am secure because of the blood Jesus shed for me. His death assures me of eternal life. It causes me to no longer dread what I miss but to focus on what's to come.

—*LaVonna Martin-Floreal, Olympics silver medalist, track*

GAME PLAN

What fears of this life get you down? Does it help to spend some time thinking about the future home in heaven that God has prepared for you?

From the Playbook:

Read Revelation 21:1–4.

SPORTS PEOPLE

ere are brief biographical notes about the sports people who contributed articles to *Power Up! for Girls.*

Kyle Abbott, baseball
Kyle is one of a number of baseball players who became major league chaplains after their careers ended. Abbott, who pitched for four years in the early 1990s (Angels, Phillies), later became the Baseball Chapel representative for the Texas Rangers.

Tricia Binford, basketball
Tricia played guard for the Utah Starzz and the Cleveland Rockers in the WNBA between 1998 and 2002. In April 2005, she was named the women's basketball coach at Montana State University. She and her husband Todd have a son, Justin.

Kim Braatz-Voisard, baseball, softball
Kim has the distinction of being the first woman to hit an over-the-fence home run against a team of professional men players. She did that in 1996 while playing for the Colorado Silver Bullets baseball team. She played centerfield for the Bullets from 1994 through 1997. Kim is married to Mark Voisard, a former pitcher in the Colorado Rockies organization.

Jenny Boucek, basketball
In 1998 Jenny was named the top basketball player in Iceland, but an injury ended her WNBA dreams early—after one year with the Cleveland Rockers. After that, she became a coach, and in 2004 she helped lead the Seattle Storm to its first WNBA title. She played college basketball at the University of Virginia where she was a two-time GTE Academic's All-American and was twice named Player of the Year. She was head coach of the Sacramento Monarchs from 2007 to 2009.

Ron Brown, football
After coaching at the University of Nebraska for two decades, Ron Brown became an assistant coach at Liberty University in 2015.

Erin Buescher Perperoglu, basketball
Erin began her college basketball career at the University of California at Santa Barbara, where she was an all-conference player. She then transferred to The Master's College to take advantage of that school's Christian atmosphere. After college, she was drafted by the Minnesota Lynx of the WNBA. She has played for Minnesota, Charlotte, and Sacramento. She also enjoys surfing and

is a member of the Christian Surfers organization. In 2006 she was named the WNBA's Most Improved Player.

Tanya Crevier, basketball
Tanya is one of the premier basketball ball-handlers in the world. Tanya played college basketball at South Dakota State, and then played in the pioneer women's pro league—the Women's Basketball League. She has been performing ball-handling shows since then, making her name known at NBA halftimes, college basketball games, and at schools and businesses.

Amanda Cromwell, soccer
At one time, Amanda was pulling off a difficult dual career as a soccer player in the WUSA and as a coach at the University of Central Florida. Before that, she was a member of the US National soccer team. She was an alternate on the 1996 team that won gold at the Olympics. Amanda began coaching Central Florida in 1999. In 2004 she was named Coach of the Year by the National Intercollegiate Soccer Officials Association. In 2013 she became the soccer coach at UCLA.

Jean Driscoll, marathons
Jean was born with spina bifida, but that did not stop her from being one of the premier athletes of the 1990s. She became a world-class wheelchair marathon champion, capturing the Boston Marathon wheelchair race eight times and winning two silver medals for the 800-meter women's wheelchair race in the Olympics. She has been awarded honorary doctorates by the University of Rhode Island and the Massachusetts School of Law and was named the Women's Sport Federation Sportswoman of the Year in 1991. She has written a book about her life, *Determined to Win*.

Tracy Hanson, golf
Tracy began her LPGA career in 1995. In 2001, she finished 44th on the LPGA money list. A graduate of San Jose State University, she lives in Ormond Beach, Florida, and has an active speaking ministry, addressing such groups as the Fellowship of Christian Athletes and College Golf Ministry.

Kedra Holland-Corn, basketball
After a successful career at Georgia, Kedra has played for Sacramento, Detroit, and Houston. Twice she averaged more than 10 points a game for the Sacramento Monarchs. On June 25, 2002, she scored a career-high 28 points in a WNBA game. She also played pro basketball overseas.

Amber Jacobs, basketball
Amber grew up around basketball, as her dad was a longtime coach and instructor. She went to Boston College and led the Lady Eagles to the NCAA Sweet 16 twice. When she graduated from BC she was the 4th leading scorer in the school's history (1,544 points). Her three-point shooting skill led to a

WNBA career. Amber was drafted by the Minnesota Lynx in 2004. In 2012 she was named women's basketball coach at Summit University of Pennsylvania.

Val Kemper, volleyball
After an All-American career on the volleyball court at Michigan State University, Val joined the US National team. She seemed destined to compete for the US women in the 2000 Olympics, but in the final weeks before the Games, she was cut from the team. That day, she had her first date with tri-athlete Hunter Kemper, whom she married in 2004.

Betsy King, golf
Betsy is a member of the LPGA Hall of Fame. During her distinguished career, she has won six majors and a total of 34 tournaments. She was named the captain of the 2007 US Solheim Cup team.

Siew-Ai Lim, golf
Born in Malaysia, Siew-Ai (See-you-I) came to the United States to attend the University of South Carolina. She stayed and now is a part of the LPGA Tour. In 2003 she finished 2nd in the Malaysian Ladies Open. On June 6, 2004, she had her biggest golf payday, finishing 2nd at the Kellogg-Keebler Classic in Illinois. She had her best year in 2004, when she finished 63rd on the Tour.

Barb Lindquist, triathlon
In college Barb competed on the Stanford swim team. In 1987 and 1991 she won gold medals in the Pan American Games. She turned a successful swim-ming career at Stanford into a wildly successful triathlon career. In 2003 she was named the No. 1 female triathlete in the world. In 2004, she competed for the US in the Olympic Games.

LaVonna Martin-Floreal, track
While competing in track for the University of Tennessee, LaVonna set school records in four events and is the all-time Lady Vol leader with 12 Southeast Conference titles. In 1992, she won the silver medal at the Olympics in the 100-meter hurdles. She competed in two Olympics for the United States. She is now a schoolteacher, and her husband, Edrick, is director of track & field at Stanford. In 2002 she was inducted into the University of Tennessee Lady Vols Hall of Fame.

Madeline Manning Mims, track
Madeline was a member of the US Olympic track team four times (1968, 1972, 1976, and 1980). She won gold in the 1968 Olympics, setting a new Olympic record in the 800-meter race (2:00.9), and she is in the National Track and Field Hall of Fame. Madeline is in full-time Christian ministry as an accomplished gospel singer and popular motivational speaker. She wrote an autobiography, *The Hope of Glory*.

Leah O'Brien-Amico, softball
Leah has earned three Olympic gold medals as a member of the US softball team. When she won gold in 2004, she was the only mom on the team. She and her husband Tommy have two children.

Leighann Reimer, basketball
Leighann was twice named the best women's college basketball player in Canada. After college she played professional basketball in Europe for three seasons. Leighann is married to Chad Reimer. They have a daughter, born in 2005. She is also the younger sister of NHL hockey star Shane Doan, a veteran player for the Arizona Coyotes.

Bill Sampen, baseball
Bill pitched in the major leagues from 1990 through 1994 with Montreal, Kansas City, and California. He finished his career with a winning record (25-21) and an ERA under 4 (3.75). After leaving baseball, he became an associate pastor of a church in Indiana.

Sue Semrau, basketball
Sue played college basketball at the University of California-San Diego, where she was the 13th top scorer in school history. When Sue Semrau took over the women's basketball team at Florida State University, the team was not very good. She turned the team around and had them in the Top 25 within three years. Sue has been named the SEC Coach of the Year and in 2001 she was voted the Atlantic Coast Conference Coach of the Year.

Charlotte Smith, basketball
Charlotte was one of the first women to dunk a basketball in college play. She will be forever remembered for hitting the winning shot in the 1995 NCAA women's basketball tournament as North Carolina won the title—one of the most exciting shots in NCAA women's basketball history. She played in both the American Basketball League and the WNBA. Charlotte spent six years with the Charlotte Sting, one with the Washington Wizards, and one with the Indiana Fever. She is now an assistant coach for her alma mater.

Wendy Ward, golf
Wendy started playing golf when she was seven years old. When she is not helping her husband Nate tend the cattle on their ranch in Washington state, Wendy is one of the top players on the LPGA Tour. Through 2005, she had won four LPGA titles. She competed twice for the US in the Solheim Cup. In 2015 she was named an assistant captain of the US Solheim Cup team.

POWER UP WRITERS

Here are brief biographical notes about the writers who contributed articles to *Power Up! for Girls*.

Rob Bentz
A longtime staff member for *Sports Spectrum* magazine, Rob is pastor of small groups at Woodmen Valley Chapel in Colorado Springs.

Dave Branon
Managing editor of *Sports Spectrum* magazine since 1990 and a contributing writer to the devotional booklet *Our Daily Bread,* Dave has written 16 books—many about Christian athletes.

Lorilee Craker
A transplanted Canadian living in Michigan, Lorilee has written several books about being a mom and other family-related issues. She has written many feature articles for *Sports Spectrum* magazine.

Dan Deal
After working as a radio producer and occasional host of *Sports Spectrum* radio at Our Daily Bread Ministries for several years, Deal left to work on the staff of Ada Bible Church in Ada, Michigan, as director of small group training and resources.

Mart DeHaan
Mart is senior content editor of Our Daily Bread Ministries. His grandfather, Dr. M. R. DeHaan, founded Radio Bible Class (now Our Daily Bread Ministries) in 1938.

Christin Ditchfield
Christin began her writing career with articles on tennis players for *Sports Spectrum*. She has written several books and has her own radio ministry, *Take It to Heart*.

Tom Felten
Tom worked with *Sports Spectrum* in a management role for a number of years. He is currently managing editor of *Our Daily Journey*, an online devotional.

Molly Ramseyer
Molly's first exposure to *Sports Spectrum* was as an intern for the magazine while she was in college. Now she serves as National Camping Director for Youth for Christ in Denver.

Brian Hettinga
Brian is the host and producer of the weekly radio program *Discover the Word*, produced by Our Daily Bread Ministries.

Jeff Olson
Jeff is a biblical counselor at Our Daily Bread Ministries. He dispenses spiritual advice to readers and listeners of Our Daily Bread publications and programs.

Roxanne Robbins
Longtime *Sports Spectrum* writer Roxanne lives in Florida when she is not working with AIDS orphans in Rwanda or Uganda. She has covered several Olympic Games for Christian media outlets. She is a regular writer for *Our Daily Journey*.